IMAGES OF
OURSELVES

IMAGES OF OURSELVES

Women with disabilities talking

Edited by
Jo Campling
Department of Social Policy, Hillcroft College

Routledge & Kegan Paul
London, Boston and Henley

First published in 1981
by Routledge & Kegan Paul Ltd
39 Store Street, London WC1E 7DD,
9 Park Street, Boston, Mass. 02108, USA and
Broadway House, Newtown Road,
Henley-on-Thames, Oxon RG9 1EN
Set in 11/13 Baskerville
and printed in Great Britain by
Billing & Sons Limited
Guildford, London, Oxford and Worcester

British Library Cataloguing in Publication Data

Images of ourselves.

1. Physically handicapped women
I. Campling, Jo
362.4'092'2   CT9983.A1   80-41986

ISBN 0-7100-0822 Pbk

Acknowledgments

My thanks to all the women with disabilities who talked to me, and especially to those who contributed to this book. My thanks to the friends who listened to me whilst I tried to work through my own experience, to Ros, Margaret, Rosemary and to Anna in Newcastle-upon-Tyne.

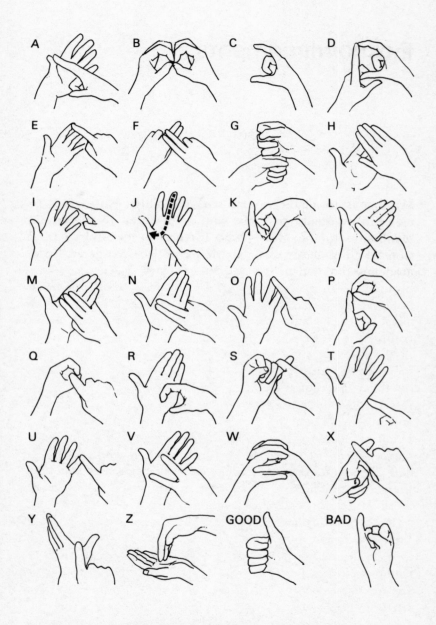

Sign language of the deaf. *See* Maggie, p.33

Introduction

In 1978 I was approached by Virago, the feminist publishers, to write a handbook for disabled women. As an able-bodied woman, I felt a certain diffidence in accepting the commission and my writing on disability had always been at the academic rather than the practical level. However, I had been brought up in a 'disabled family' since my mother had had polio at the age of three and I was enthusiastic about the aims of the 'Handbook' series and so I accepted. After completing *Better Lives*, I got to know a large number of disabled women, far in excess of those who originally helped me with it, mostly through letters, comments and reviews on the book. Some of them had become close friends. My reservations increased and, more significantly, my attitude and my feelings began to change radically. It was not that I felt my authorship necessarily inappropriate within the narrow terms of reference of a handbook, but rather that it had been a tentative, often inadequate beginning and that there was much more to be said in a more personal framework. Hence this collection.

I asked my friends to write whatever they wanted about their situations as women with disabilities. I rejected the idea of interviews because even the most skilful interviewer cannot help but be directive. I did not want the impromptu answer but deeply felt, considered contribution. I have written the briefest of introductions to each piece, simply to give a framework in which the reader can place the writer. I have limited the editorial function to the minimum and I have not presumed to make a commentary or interpretation. The contributions speak for themselves; anything else would be superfluous and an intrusion. Spontaneously, and without plan, all the themes which I identified in *Better Lives* emerge — personal relationships, sexuality, motherhood, education and employment as well as the practical issues such as benefits, clothing and so on. However, most of all, the writers tell us about attitudes towards women with disabilities, about their position in society and, by reflection, our own dilemma as able-bodied women.

The contributors range from adolescence to old age, from a wide variety of backgrounds and from all over the country. Several are friends but the majority do not know each other. Some are feminists, some would question the use of the word, and some would reject it altogether. Some could only write with the physical help of other women. They are not professional writers, although some have written for publication before and two have published books. What they do have in common is that they are all women with disabilities.

The original plan of action for the United Nations Decade for Women, 1975-1985, included the intention to study measures which would help disabled women lead more fulfilling lives, but for various reasons it was dropped. 1981 is the International Year of Disabled Persons, whose major aim is to promote the full participation of *all* disabled people in society. We will see. Micheline says, 'I cannot pinpoint when I first began to listen to the experiences of able-bodied women and relate them to my own.' Able-bodied women must be able to do this. We must learn to recognise our own attitudes towards disability, relate to our experiences, isolate our guilt, and work positively on our feelings. Micheline again, 'I realised how strong women are, especially when we have to fight to overcome something, in our case our disabilities.' This book is for all of us.

Jo Campling

SARAH

Sarah, who is 17, lives with her parents in Surrey. She is hemiplegic with restricted movement on one side. She has two brothers and one sister, all older and able-bodied. Originally she attended an ordinary school but, at her own request, transferred to the Thomas Delarue Spastic School at Tonbridge. She has 3 'O' levels and has been accepted at Queen Elizabeth College at Leatherhead to do a course in business studies. She is a very able swimmer and has won several medals and certificates.

As the youngest child, born with a disability, I am very lucky to have a caring family. I have a particularly good relationship with the younger of my two brothers. He helped me to become more independent by fighting with me so I had to defend myself and become stronger. I always felt that my sister and brothers were more intelligent than I was. I worked hard at school but never seemed to achieve their standards and this began to undermine my confidence. My disability restricts me only to the extent that if I want to achieve something, I have to work twice as hard as an able-bodied person. Then what I do achieve may not be perfect but I persist and do not give up. There are some things that I just cannot do like gymnastics and ballet dancing. I can sew but so slowly that it bores me to do it.

When I was at junior school I never had nasty comments

1

about my disability. It was probably because when children are very young they don't notice that a disabled person is any different from anyone else. The local integrated comprehensive school was a different matter altogether. I felt very self-conscious about my disability because both the other girls and the teachers made it difficult for me. The students did not treat me as a girl with a slight handicap but as a person set apart. I felt that I was worthless and very vulnerable every time someone made a personal remark to me or about me. They used to ask questions like 'Why can't you go to the disco?' (It was four miles away.) I would say that I didn't want to go and they would whisper and giggle. Then I would remain quiet and hurt inside. I did have a sort of friend there but I would not call her a friend now because she had a bad reputation with the rest of the class and was very unpopular. I felt we were in the same situation in different ways. She used to make me do errands for her, like carrying her bag up four flights of stairs as some sort of threat that if I did not she would not be my friend. Once she made me kiss the toilet floor and then told everyone that I had done it voluntarily and I was very embarrassed. She used to tell me that she had a new boyfriend every week. I went along with these stories until she made up false telephone numbers and pretended to talk to them. I knew they were false because when I asked to listen she said they were cut off. I didn't have any boyfriends and used to wait hours for her and then get home very late. The other girls just ignored me and I felt very isolated. They didn't want to be seen with a handicapped girl especially when their boyfriends were around. It was not only the girls who gave me a tough time but the teachers as well. They were not sure how to treat me, particularly in the sporting activities. And most of them did not give me much encouragement academically. I began to lose all confidence in myself and became very unhappy and depressed. I wanted to be a part of the group but I could not see how to join in. I used to feel that no one else could be as isolated as

I was in that huge school.

I wondered what it would be like to be in a school for handicapped people. I felt that a special school might be my only escape. No one suggested this solution to me as everyone thought that I could manage perfectly well in an ordinary school. I had a long talk with my father and he understood. For two years he tried to get me into a special school. When the other girls found out what was happening they teased me and said I would be a moron if I went to a handicapped school. Eventually I got a place at the Thomas Delarue School in Kent, which was a boarding school for disabled children. I can remember my last night at home very clearly. I had a terrifying nightmare of lots of very severely handicapped people (more handicapped than I had ever seen or imagined) crowding round me in a circle, telling me that I did not belong to them. Then they tried to bury me with all their strange aids and appliances. It was very frightening and I did not know what to expect. I need not have worried at all because I found out that I could get on with them much better. Although on the first night, when I was put into a dormitory with three girls, one of whom was very severely handicapped, I thought that my nightmare was coming true. She has now become my friend.

It was a vastly different world at Thomas Delarue. It was much easier to make friends and I didn't feel an outsider any more. Everyone had a disability and no one was self-conscious about it. They treated each other as human beings and you could be friends with anyone. Some of the pupils had very restricted speech. It was like learning a new, strange language but when I got used to it I was patient enough to understand them. With them I did not ask long questions but ones which had multiple choice answers so that they could reply and we got along fine. I now have a few special friends who are so close that they are like sisters to me. My best friend is more disabled than I am and she is in a wheelchair, but she helps me just as much as I help her but in different ways. I have now lost touch with the people from the other school and even the girls at the Guides. I am rather sad about this as it means I have no contact with the outside world. I sometimes think now that if I met someone from the old days I would be happy and overwhelmed to see them whatever response they gave me in return. I have the feeling that I shall always be lonely inside.

LISA

Lisa, who is 18, was born with bilateral myelodisplacia and can only walk with crutches. She is studying for 'A' levels at the Lord Mayor Treloar College in Hampshire and from there goes out daily to courses at the local sixth form college. During vacations she lives at home with her parents in Middlesex. Lisa hopes to go on to university to do business or computer studies. She took part in the BBC TV series 'The Handicapped Family'.

In this world in which physical perfection is sought by the majority of women, and which is given so much publicity in many circles of society, it is obvious that those who are, in one way or another, physically disabled will often be regarded as 'different', and will have many difficulties in making those around them aware that in fact they are the same in most other aspects as other women. One of my greatest problems is in making people accept me for what I am — an individual, to make them realise that although I am disabled, I am capable of leading a 'normal' life and doing exactly the same things as I would have done otherwise.

In my opinion one of the most important facts that some people seem to disregard is that although physically different, mentally I am not disabled. I share the same hopes, anxieties, fears and general emotions with women the world over. Many people have supposed that because I am obviously disabled I am mentally sub-normal and have therefore treated me as they would someone of low intelligence or as a child. When I was young this did not upset me much, but to treat an eighteen-year-old as a young child is not only degrading and upsetting but deeply embarassing. It therefore becomes more important for me to be able to show people that I am capable of living a 'normal' life by mixing with them in the same social places and by competing with them in every aspect of it, socially, academically and in leisure pursuits.

At first the actual meeting with people who were not disabled was difficult. I attend a boarding college for handicapped students where I lead a varied social life but the main difficulties arise during the holidays when I find that I know very few people of my own age in the locality and find it extremely hard to socialise because of this. I am just getting over feelings of shyness, inferiority and insecurity which have, in the past, made it even harder for me to go out and meet people. Now I am realising that if I am to go out and lead a fulfilling life I must have personal confidence, for it is only through self-confidence you can make others around you relax in your company and come to accept you as a friend.

Quite often I find that there is the added problem of the wheelchair or crutches becoming a psychological barrier between the outside world and the disabled person. They are obvious and the user is quickly registered as 'a disabled person'. This barrier is often difficult to break down and it usually takes time and patience before you are accepted as a normal human being and the disability disregarded. Some people say that 'you can't tell a book by its cover'; this is a very nice ideal, but in reality the cover — the person's physical appearance — is always judged before their personality, and first impressions are formed on the information that the senses send to the brain. It is therefore more important that I create a good impression not only visually but personality-wise if I am to compensate for any flaws there may be physically.

Some people have been surprised at the varied social life that I lead, but like any other person of my age this is a very important aspect of my life. The theatre, cinema and many other places hold the same interest for me as they do for others. They also provide a means by which I am able to come into contact with 'the outside world' and to integrate in it. Here, however, there are also problems with access in many buildings. It is true that all modern buildings are being designed to cater for the disabled but many, particularly older ones, are totally inaccessible, or, for reasons concerned with fire precautions, we are not admitted. In many theatres and cinemas the disabled are seen as acute fire risks, they would apparently be too slow to vacate the building in the event of fire, or would need such help that they would be endangering the lives of others, yet many people I know, including myself, would be capable of leaving a burning building under their own steam, perhaps faster than some able-bodied people could. In some theatres that I have visited, I have been provided with my own personal 'companion' who has insisted on pushing me to my seat and creating such a fuss that my presence in the theatre has become too obvious and rather embarrassing. I am in no way saying that their help should not be provided for those who need it, but that it should be provided on asking and not automatically because you are disabled. Many disabled people handle their wheelchairs better than anyone else, so the helper can become more of a hindrance than a help.

I am very interested in sport, including canoeing, swimming, archery and various others. In my opinion not enough handicapped people know about the facilities that there are, or could be, for this type of activity. Some people think that there is too much risk involved in such sports as canoeing and swimming, but providing that the disability is not too severe and correct coaching can be obtained there is no more risk for the disabled person than for the non-disabled.

The college that I attend gives a lot of encouragement to those who compete in any sports. It is a pity that more schools and colleges do not follow their example. I am also very lucky in having parents who have always encouraged me to compete in new sports and who have seen that the risks involved are no greater because I am disabled. Not only do sports provide exercise, but also another way in which I can meet and compete with people as an equal. In canoeing I have the same advantages as able-bodied people as I only have to use my body above the waist and in some respects I have the added advantage of strength in my arms due to the continued use of crutches and wheelchairs. I now attend an ordinary canoe club where I find that my disability does not limit me at all. It becomes more of a challenge for me to do ambitious things. For example I canoed with a party of equally disabled girls down a French river with fast moving water, rapids and waterfalls, which probably had I not been disabled I would never have done.

All disabled people must be able to mix freely with able-bodied people if they are to become as independent as possible but there is always the added problem of transportation from place to place. This has to be overcome before a disabled person can be employed as usually there are distances between home and work. Up to a certain point one can rely upon others for transportation but I find this very limiting as you can only go out when others are free to take you, therefore your independence is being cut. At one time, because I find using public transport difficult, I had to rely upon taxi services when away from home and upon my parents when I was at home — the former became very expensive and although I am very grateful to my parents, there will be a time in the future when I will not have them to rely upon. I have now solved my problems by learning to drive my own second-hand car which I run using my 'mobility allowance'. I could have used the 'motability scheme' which meant giving up my mobility allowance, but by either method some form of personal transport must be obtained if full independence is to be reached.

I try to live a normal active life. I am lucky in a way that I was born disabled and so have not had to adjust to a new way of life, just to overcome any problems that the disability has caused naturally. The greatest help which can be given to disabled people, like myself, is a greater public awareness of our needs in access, transport and other aspects of daily living. With this is needed the realisation not only of the disability but of the capabilities of the individual, and an acceptance that there are no disabled people. We are just people who happen to use crutches or wheelchairs but we are otherwise no different to the rest of society.

ANGIE

Angie, who is 21, lived in residential care for fifteen years, but two years ago moved to an adapted flat with her husband. She has cerebral palsy, which means she is unable to walk and gets around in an electric wheelchair. She works as a clerical assistant for the Department of the Environment. She wants to travel to as many places as possible and in a few years would like to have children.

From the age of six years old I attended a residential school for disabled children. The school was very poor on education, so much so that at the age of sixteen I was only at the level of a nine-year-old. I used to go home at weekends and talk to the able-bodied kids about what they were doing at school. I had never even heard of some of the subjects they studied. I felt so ashamed that they knew more than I did and I was a lot older. I decided to ask my teacher why I did not do the same things as my friends did at their school. She told me it was because I was disabled and that there wasn't much point in educating me to 'O' and 'A' level as I would never get a job. I told her I was not prepared to spend my life in a workshop making baskets. I was going to improve my education and get a job in open employment no matter how long it took. Since the age of twelve I had been very bored with school life and started to become rebellious. I felt frustrated and couldn't explain why. Most of the other children were not very intelligent and this made me feel very alone. I could not talk to them as friends. I tried to talk to some of the staff about how I felt, but in their eyes we were all the same whatever disability we had. I was told to go and play and stop bothering them. This was quite common amongst the staff, never explaining what their ideas meant. One idea which most of the staff held was explained to me quite clearly. I was about four-teen years old and had just finished preparing a salad in the cookery class. The teacher came over and said, 'What a good job you have made of that. You would have made someone a good wife.' 'What do you mean, I would have?' I asked. 'Well', she replied, 'What I meant to say was if you marry a disabled man, you would make him a good wife.' The school had really strange ideas on marriage and the disabled. They believed that if a disabled person got married it should be to another disabled person as it would not be fair on an able-bodied person to burden them with a handicapped partner. Anyway an able-bodied person would not fancy a disabled person. I didn't go along with this idea at all. I knew for a fact that able-bodied boys fancied me. I had proved that when I went home for weekends.

They also seemed to think that disabled people did not have any feelings. Well, that was how it seemed to me. I remember a humiliating experience I had when I was twelve. It was in the physiotherapy room. I was seeing the doctor who came from the local hospital on weekly visits. On this particular day he had brought five male student doctors with him, and I was made to walk naked in front of them and then lie on a mat while in turn they examined my body, opening and closing my legs, poking and prodding here and there and making comments. I was at the age when I was developing from a child into a woman and they made me feel so embarrassed. I used to cry on these visits. Then I started to lose respect for my body but it wasn't so embarrassing for me. There was no one I could talk to mainly because I was too young to understand what was happening. I had learned how to defend myself from an early age. I had to be strong minded and strong willed and by the age of fourteen I started to respect my body again. It took a long time and even today I sometimes find it difficult.

I left school when I was sixteen and went to live at a centre for adults. At the centre I tried to improve my education but this was very difficult. The other people at the centre were of normal intelligence and I easily made friends. When I'd been living there for a year I met and fell in love with a member of staff, a care assistant. His name was Tony and he came from my home county. We found we had quite a lot in common and enjoyed each other's company. Before Tony and I got together some of the staff tried to discourage me from going out with him. In the centre, such relationships were frowned upon because most of the staff did not approve of them. However, after a while our relationship developed and each day Tony was doing more things for me. Then he moved into my room and we started living together. This was made easy for us because firstly, as we were living away from home we didn't have any parental pressure and also we did not have the problem of finding somewhere to live. Secondly, the Principal, unlike most of the staff, realised that disabled people had the same feelings as anyone else so he allowed us to be together. Tony had looked after handicapped people for some time so he knew what was involved and anyway we loved each other so we found it easy to adapt.

We lived at the centre for fifteen months and then got married. We lived a further four months there and then we moved to our flat. It is a ground-floor flat which has been adapted to my needs. Tony got a new job and I stayed at home alone. At first I was very lonely as I had never been without people, having always lived in residential establishments. I spent most of my time trying to become more independent and on one occasion I sat on the loo for three hours until Tony came home from work. I just could not get off and I felt so angry with myself but there was nothing I could do. When Tony came home he was worried when I told him how long I had been sitting there. When he realised that I was OK we started to laugh as it was quite funny. At first Tony had wanted to give up his job and stay at home to look after me but he knew it was better for us if he could work and if I could be as independent as possible. Nowadays he doesn't worry because I am really quite independent.

When we had been living in our flat for some weeks, my Mum rang and told me she had met the headmaster of my old school, who had asked about me. She told him that I was now married and living in a flat. He asked what handicap my husband had. When my Mum told him Tony was able-bodied he was quite surprised and didn't know what to say. I have met a number of people who seemed surprised when they find out Tony is not disabled. It is as if they cannot understand how an able-bodied man can marry a disabled girl. One day while Tony was at work the gas man came to read the meter. I showed him where it was and waited in the doorway for him to finish. I always sit with the door open when anyone I don't know comes to the flat, in case they try anything, so I can shout to my neighbour who lives upstairs. As he was leaving the flat he turned and asked if I was married? I told him I was, then a funny look came into his eyes and he asked if I had sex? I was shocked at his question and at first was stuck for words. Then I was angry and said the first thing that came into my head. 'Yes, do you?' He looked embarassed and hurried away. During the rest of the day I kept thinking what a cheek he had asking me such a question. Since then I have been asked that question several times in different ways, most often by men, and I answer them in the same way. But some people do seem genuinely concerned. For instance, I had some builders in doing some adaptations. One of them was very fatherly and friendly and we had long chats over cups of tea. He was about forty and was married with five children. One day he tried to ask me if I had sex but couldn't find the right words. I knew what he was getting at so I told him not to worry as everything was all right and we were very happy that way. For the rest of the day he never stopped apologising for asking such a personal question. Somehow I did not mind him asking as I felt he was not just curious but anxious about us.

Tony and I are often asked if we are brother and sister. The first time we were asked this was while we were buying some fruit and the shop assistant asked Tony. He replied, 'No, Angie is my wife.' The man seemed really surprised and stared long and hard at me. We left him thinking it over! The next occasion stands out clearly in my mind because of the fuss leading up to it. We were in a restaurant enjoying our meal when we noticed all the waiters watching us. We ignored them hoping they would lose interest but they didn't. Eventually one came over and whispered to Tony, 'Is she your sister?' When Tony said I was his wife, he looked quite incredulous and went off to tell the others. We couldn't help laughing, to think that was why they were standing watching us trying to find the courage to ask us.

Questions like these used to bother us but after a while we learned how to handle them. It would be better though if people would stop and think before they spoke and try and put themselves in our place. How would they feel if someone asked them if they had sex? Or if the person with them is their sister or brother? Why shouldn't disabled and able-bodied people be lovers and marry?

EDWINA

Edwina, who is 24 years old, has cerebral palsy. Her speech is restricted and she is in a wheelchair. She has a younger brother and sister who live at home with her parents. She met Derek, who is able-bodied and works as an assistant cost surveyor with a building firm. They have been married for a year and live in a flat in South London. She belongs to the Support Group for People with Disabilities and is a Council Member of GLAID.

Edwina's contribution was dictated to Micheline.

When I was born the doctors thought I would die because I was so small and I stopped breathing at the time of birth. The consequences were that the lack of oxygen caused cerebral palsy which, at the time, no one knew. About six months later when babies are starting to co-ordinate their hands and sitting up, I didn't. My parents took me to our GP and he sent us to Great Ormond Street to see a paediatrician and he said that I had brain damage which causes cerebral palsy. It must have been a great shock to both parents that their pretty little girl was going to be different and this had a bad effect on their marriage. They divorced. My mother wanted me to be put into a home, but my father and family wouldn't have this, so we went to live with my grandparents. My father heard of the hospital in Cheyne Walk in Chelsea so off we went to see what could be done. I can remember being pulled about by the physiotherapist and being filmed with nothing on. This ritual went on for the next few years then one day I realised I didn't want to be filmed in this way. It was as if I had no sex. So I progressed at Cheyne Walk, my co-ordination improving and my family and father becoming more protective. It was decided that while my Dad and his fiancée got to know each other I should stay in the hostel from Monday to Friday. I didn't like this because I wanted to be at home and I used to kick up quite a fuss. But when they got married my stepmother

had me home. I remember at that time that I dribbled a
lot and my mother tried to dress me up. I was so nervous
about spoiling the clothes that it became worse. As a little
girl I remember that I thought to myself that when I grew
up I wouldn't dribble, I wouldn't make a mess when I fed
myself and my speech would be perfect. I went to a day
school in Kingston for five years where I was taught to walk
with calipers. I hated those calipers because my dresses never
covered them up. I had this craze that every time I dribbled
I wanted to change my dress but my mother kept saying,
'You can't because of the washing.' I remember the headmaster saying to visitors that it's such a pity that she's bright
because not a lot of people can understand her.

I went to boarding school and because there were people
there who had faith in me, they pushed me to do my best.
This sowed the seed of bloody-mindedness. If someone
said I couldn't do something I would go all out to prove them
wrong. I made up my mind then that I wanted an operation
to stop me dribbling. I bullied the doctors until they gave
me the operation I wanted. I felt a lot more confident
after this. I was quite popular at school because I helped
them make fun of me. Because I was jolly. This was what I
call a put-at-ease theory, i.e. I used to put people at their
ease at my own cost. This is best explained in my college and
later days. If I wanted a particular guy to like me I would
put him at his ease by letting him think that I was a bubbling,
noisy, don't-worry-nothing-hurts-me person. It was like
saying 'treat me like one of the boys.' At that time I had a
lot of confidence as a person, but not much as a woman.
I thought that I was not very attractive because of my speech,
and I couldn't get witty remarks out at the right time. When I
went to parties where I didn't know anyone, I would sit in an
ordinary chair and not move or speak and men would come
and chat me up, but as soon as I spoke they would often turn
away or go and get a drink and not come back. When I went
with some man that I knew, I felt protected and, if I could
get away with it, I wouldn't talk too much.

I went to live back with my parents and got a volunteer job with a charity. My theory was still in practice and I was very nervous and up-tight because my father and my family were very protective and wouldn't let me do anything in the house. I had this feeling of being trapped and relationships outside the home began to suffer. The volunteer job stopped and under great pressure from my parents and social services, I went to a work centre run by the Spastics Society. I felt it was very degrading putting things into bags, and my fellow workers and I seemed to have nothing in common. At that time I decided to get a flat, to my parents' horror. Once I made up my mind I was given a flat with a warden to call if I needed help. So I moved. I felt very scared because I had never cooked before for myself and I thought, 'What if I burn myself?' I was very lonely at first but enjoyed finding out what I could do. Every day I accomplished something new. Such a lot happened in that time. Derek crashed into my life and I didn't use my theory because I think he would have seen through it. Our relationship seemed to escalate. In no time we were thinking about getting married. Our friends were not surprised but both sets of parents were horrified. My father said that we could get engaged but not married and Derek's mother said, 'Why do you want to marry her, she's in a wheelchair?' I was angry. They were both trying to take my rights as a woman away from me. Luckily Derek didn't listen to them and after a lot of hassle all round we married. So far it's working out just fine.

JULIE

Julie, who is 25 years old, lives with her parents in Hertford-shire. She was badly injured in a car accident when she was 18 and is now tetraplegic, paralysed from the armpits down-wards. She is confined to her wheelchair and is incontinent

and severely hypothermic. She has studied with the Open
University and writes for *Spare Rib*. Last year she and her
mother travelled to Africa. She has three boyfriends but
says she is short on girlfriends.

If a disabled woman is unable to go out to work she is at
a great disadvantage in terms of meeting other people.
During weekdays when I see young women leaving for and
returning from work, I feel quite apart from the outside
world. Whatever activities you take up, whether it is painting
or an Open University degree, nobody can convince you that
it is the same as being active within a normal work situation.
This can make you feel inadequate both physically and
mentally, especially if you worked prior to disability. If
you have boyfriends, girlfriends or a husband, it is extremely
difficult to join in a discussion of their working day. Sometimes I find myself switching off or disappearing into the
corner of the room. The outcome can be self-destructive.
It helps if you take an interest in your partner's or friend's
career. Even if it is just a case of making the appropriate
noises! But equally they must take an interest in your daily
activities.

Encounters at parties or other social functions vary, but
tend to follow certain patterns. One is complete rejection,
where even eye contact is impossible, because people are
embarrassed or indifferent and you are written off. Another
is over-enthusiasm, when you may be treated as a novelty and
the fact that you are the only wheelchair guest can draw
excess attention, not so much for yourself but your situation. Sometimes you receive too much admiration, often
from older, married men, who will then pour out all their
troubles. Often, promises are made at the end of what may
seem a fruitful evening but will you ever see him again?
Even if sincere at the time, parties can be a superficial basis
for a relationship.

Personal relationships can be difficult if you live with your
parents, in a 'disabled family'. (I define this as a family whose

existence revolves around the disabled member. My mother gave up a highly paid career to care for me, thus leaving a greater financial burden on my father. Unfortunately state benefits and services can't bridge this financial gap.) The situation can be frustrating if you are at the age, as I am, when you would be living independently, working and travelling. Parents can be over-protective. They may interrogate your partner more than in normal circumstances because after all you are more vulnerable to maltreatment. You are unable to create your own atmosphere in such a situation — making coffee, or just moving around. In intimate relationships there is also that first moment when the mechanics of your bladder management are revealed. This is the major test. How will he react to a mature woman who wears plastic knickers, pads and requires help when going to the loo? Rejection on this count is painful and inhibiting. If your relationship passes the bladder test, the next hurdle is arranging a time and a private meeting place. Time is an important factor because a considerable amount of physical preparation is required for intercourse and unexpected visitors or disturbances are impossible to cope with. The disabled person is unable to quickly get up, dress, wash. Even when sexually aroused, the spontaneity can soon disappear when your partner has to help empty your bladder and carefully clean and position you. Overexhaustion, especially if orgasm is achieved, can make the disabled woman feel inadequate. The mind may be willing to try out new positions and experiences, but the body function is that much weaker. I suppose we all have sexual fantasies. Mine relate to spontaneous sexual behaviour — sex in a lift, in any room of the house, and in numerous positions, on the floor, up against the wall, etc. A successful sexual relationship is impossible to define. If you are praised, there is always a feeling of doubt. No one can really convince you of sexual prowess when half your body isn't really normal. You may also worry about your body shape. Most disabilities come equipped with drooping breasts, a thin rib-cage and a lax tum, due to lack of muscle-tone. You may compare your body shape with how it was prior to disability and wonder whether your partner is comparing your body to someone else's. The inability of the disabled person to be purely physical, showing body movement, posture, wearing attractive clothes, can be a great disadvantage within the 'market place' of relationships. Seeing such physical abilities in others can result in jealousy which is hard to admit. To compensate in some way I sometimes find myself putting on a front, pushing my personality and 'sitting pretty' in order to be noticed. This can be exhausting and humiliating.

I think that cultural differences can play a great part in attitudes towards disability. During a trip to Kenya I was pleasantly surprised and relieved by the black Kenyans' attitudes. Many asked frankly and intelligently whether sitting in a wheelchair was caused by illness or an accident. Once the problems were explained, it was a case of 'okay no problem'. They looked upon my disability realistically, no psychological hang-ups. This seems part of a fatalistic philosophy absent in the West, plus natural acceptance of daily hardships. 'Okay, so you wear baby-type knickers but everyone has their problems,' said a black male friend, who found me mentally and physically attractive. Our relationship involved minimal pushing on my part and I felt really relaxed.

'Is your boyfriend a nurse or homosexual?' This question has been put to me (or implied) many times. It always annoys me since it implies a prejudice against homosexuality and also that it is unnatural for a male to take on a caring role. Essentially in a media-orientated society, caring goes against the male macho image and certainly research has shown that disabled men have a greater chance of marrying able-bodied women than the other way round. Perhaps with greater sexual equality and a more flexible attitude towards male and female roles, as husbands, as wives, as breadwinners, as carers, this will no longer be the case. But at the back of my mind there is always the question 'Will any man take on the responsibility for me as a severely disabled woman that my parents have?'

SU

Su, who is 25 years old, was born in Newcastle-upon-Tyne. She has spina bifida, which has resulted in her being paraplegic. She was educated at home until she attended Walbottle Grammar School from the age of 12. Su went on to the University of Newcastle-upon-Tyne where she obtained a BA (Hons) in Politics. From there she moved to Manchester University to do postgraduate work and was awarded an MA. She is now working for her doctorate at Newcastle University.

An increasing number of people now subscribe to the notion that being both female *and* disabled is a double handicap. Is this a valid analysis, or are male paraplegics, for example, treated in the same way as women who are paraplegics — and so on? In my experience, I believe that the former is probably true — for instance, people will often rush to help me in putting my wheelchair into my car, yet if I were a man, they would probably be far more reluctant to assist, the male ego being such a fragile blossom! If only people would realise my muscles are almost as well-developed as those of a Russian discus-thrower! This leads one to the conclusion that the age-old cliché of men treating women as beings which should be cosseted and pampered is compounded when that same woman happens to be disabled. I believe that most disabled people have to possess a certain amount of aggression in order to achieve some degree of independence — it would possibly be stretching the point to say that most successful women are aggressive, and therefore a disabled woman must be doubly aggressive. However, it would be true to say that

had I been a disabled man, I would still have been determined
to attain my independence, but being born a woman may
have given that facet of my personality a sharper fighting
edge.

The problem of discrimination is just as complex. When
I left the University of Manchester after completing my postgraduate studies, I found it very difficult to obtain employment. This could have been due to one of three factors:
my lack of experience in most of the jobs for which I
applied; my disability; the fact that I am a woman. Or
could it have been a combination of all three? I am sure that
some discrimination in terms of sex and/or disability did
exist — this is underlined by the fact that most application
forms ask (a) the sex of the applicant, and (b) whether the
applicant is disabled. When being interviewed, my disability
was always mentioned — for instance, how mobile was I —
would I be able to cope with the work? This is as ridiculous
as asking a person with red hair whether they could cope
with the work, and whether the colour of their hair would
affect their performance — one wouldn't apply for the job
if one was unsure about coping. The only interview at which
I wasn't asked any of these patronising questions was when
I was recently interviewed for a studentship at the University
of Newcastle — it could be significant that my application
was successful. The panel concerned obviously took into
account that I had completed a full-time degree at Newcastle, and then a year's postgraduate work at Manchester,
and weren't influenced, as many academics are, by the still-
prevalent concept that women don't make serious academics.

In terms of personal relationships, I have never found my
disability a problem. True, many people still wonder — in
suitably hushed tones — whether it is possible for a disabled
person to enjoy sex. On the other hand, I think that some
men are fascinated by the idea of having sex with a disabled
woman — perhaps they see it as an interesting variation!
But even when not enjoying a fulfilling relationship with a
member of the opposite sex, this doesn't worry me unduly —

I believe my attitude would be the same if I weren't a paraplegic, since at the moment my career is far too important for me, and any heavy relationships would probably be an unnecessary digression. That's not to say that I am a totally unfeeling person, but I don't think that managing to hook a man is the only way a woman can find fulfilment. This brings me neatly to the matter of marriage and children. My personal feelings are that I wouldn't want to be married and have a family — marriage is now redundant (for me at least). In addition, I don't think I would ever have the urge to rear children, partly for practical reasons — there is a strong possibility that spina bifida is hereditary — partly for the reason that I value my independence — I don't think I could invest as much of myself as is needed in order to bring up children properly. However, I do think that if a disabled woman wants to have children, then nothing should stop her, despite the fact that some people still find this totally unacceptable. Perhaps this is due to the reactionary views of some people based on the elimination of the weaker elements from society — but that is another argument in itself.

I sometimes think that women in general find it easier to accept a disability, since it is still a widely accepted norm that women are dependent on men economically. When a man becomes disabled to such an extent that it prevents him from filling his role as breadwinner, he must find this much harder to accept. But when a woman becomes disabled (I am referring here to people who have once been completely fit and mobile), although she may find it hard to come to terms with the fact that she may not be able to carry out all the tasks she could once perform, the position of woman as dependent on man would seem to lead to a greater degree of acceptance. However, I do not think this is necessarily a good thing if it makes a woman even more dependent both economically and physically on her husband, for example.

Although attitudes towards disabled people are changing —

albeit slowly — there is still a long way to go. Many people still do not realise that inside a body sitting in a wheelchair there is usually a lively mind waiting to express itself and show that disabled person to be every bit as independent as the able-bodied majority. For independence is not just a physical thing — it is a state of mind, it is saying, 'I want to do something, and even if it takes me a bit longer and I may have to ask for help if I need it, I'm going to do it.' The crucial thing here is asking for help if it is *needed* — people often assume that I am helpless, even when doing something simple, such as pushing myself along the street. If I need help I will ask, but if I am offered it and I don't need it, I will usually politely refuse. Perhaps disabled men have the same problem, but the fact that it is usually men who offer me assistance makes me wonder if more women offer disabled men assistance!

Finally, a few words on condescension. Occasionally, people 'talk down' to me — again, is this because I am a woman, or because I am disabled, or both? When they find out that I have been to university, they often express admiration and wonderment — 'How marvellous', they say — why is it marvellous? Just because I can't use my legs doesn't mean that I have performed some superhuman feat in managing to attend some lectures and sitting a few exams — after all, I use my hands to write, and my brains to answer the questions set in exams, not my legs! This problem is something which faces both men and women who happen to be disabled, and who have achieved some measure of success, both in their careers and their personal lives. But until the role of women in society is viewed differently, the role of disabled women cannot be totally transformed. Since women are still seen as the 'weaker sex', it logically follows that the disabled (especially disabled women) will continue to be seen as the weaker and less able members of society. Therefore, I conclude that the total acceptance of disabled people as no different from anyone else in society is necessarily connected with the equality of the sexes in society.

MICHELINE

Micheline was born in 1950 with a congenital disability called osteogenesis imperfecta (brittle bones). She spent most of her first four years in hospital, but gradually her bones lost their fragility and by the age of 10 the periods in hospital had come to an end. Nevertheless during these ten years she had had over forty major fractures. Micheline had home tutors as special schools were not willing to have a child with her disability and the education authorities were not keen to send her as they said she was 'too intelligent'. She passed her 11+ and won a place at the county grammar school, who were also not willing to accept her. At the age of 14 she went to the Florence Treloar Boarding School, the first grammar school for girls with disabilities to open in this country. She left with 6 'O' levels and 2 'A' levels and went to Art College for three years. She realised that commercial art was not going to suit her and eventually went to work for a small charity, first as a volunteer and later as assistant to the director. During this period she left home and went to live in a bedsitter. She resigned from her job in order to preserve her own integrity and started her own association — GLAID. In 1979 she published a book, *Creating Your Own Work*. Micheline studied re-evaluation co-counselling which she now teaches. Using these skills, she initiated and now co-leads the London Support Group for People with Disabilities.

Animals have it easy. I mean, for example, that it is very unlikely that a horse wastes much time wondering if she is really a horse, whilst human beings seem disposed to spending vast amounts of totally unproductive time wondering if they are really human beings at all. Well, some do.

The first time the doubt that I belonged to this particular planet struck me, was a glorious, calm, blue-skied day when I was twelve years old. Lying flat on my back in the garden, staring at the sky, I was thinking about growing up. Until that moment I think I had somehow believed that when I grew up I would become 'normal', i.e. without a disability. 'Normal' then meant to me, 'like my big sister', pretty, rebellious, going out with boys, doing wonderful, naughty things with them, leaving school and getting a job, leaving home, getting married and having children. That momentous day I suddenly realised that my life was not going to be like that at all. I was going to be just the same as I had always been — very small, funnily shaped, unable to walk. It seemed at that moment that the sky cracked. My vision expanded wildly. My simply black and white world exploded into vivid colours which dazzled and frightened me in a way in which I had never been frightened before. Everything familiar took on an ominous hue. At that point I saw life, especially with regard to other women, as a huge competition, and I believed that I was just not equipped to compete. My girl-friend from next door came out and suggested a game as she had done many times before. I remember her look of confusion and hurt when I said I didn't want to play any more.

The next two years seemed like a dark roller-coaster ride, sometimes happy, often plunging into despair. My main preoccupation seemed to be desperately trying to deny the awareness of my difference which had started on that day. I spent hours making my hair seem 'right', playing with make-up, fighting with my parents to wear the clothes that were fashionable, studying the 'pop' charts, talking in what I fondly imagined would be with-it language, looking in the mirror to check on my developing shape, hoping that puberty would alter my body past all recognition. It didn't. It just added a few bulges here and there and gave me period pains. No one seemed to understand or be interested in what I was going through. 'She's trying to be like everyone else', was one comment I remember very clearly. I filled in for myself the silent, 'but she isn't'. Sex was distinctly not talked about. Nor was the issue of my having children which I had started to worry about from that day onwards. I dared not ask anyone for help because I knew they could not give me the help I wanted. People said to me that I would accept, in time, my restricted life. They said that I had many things to be thankful for, such as my talent for drawing which I would no doubt develop so that I could work at home and derive all my satisfaction from Art. I just wanted to be told that I was beautiful and that everything would be all right.

I guess when you go about feeling like a mouldy artichoke, people tend to react to you as though you were one. I was so shy, especially with boys, that very few managed to over-come their reactions to my disability and my self-consciousness enough for any conversation to last more than five minutes, thus affirming my belief that I was unlovable. However, one or two confident souls broke through to me despite all this. I experienced my first real kiss when I was fourteen. I didn't like it much, but I think from that moment on the grey clouds began to part. At some point during those two years, I worked out that the cosy future my family had planned for me would be so boring that I would rather die than make their gloomy prophesies come true. When the chance came for me to go to a boarding school for girls with disabilities, I jumped at it. I saw it as the beginning of my road to freedom.

Our boarding school had rows of adjacent loos. One day, very soon after my arrival at the school. I was sitting in one loo whilst a new friend was sitting in the loo next door. 'Micheline,' she said, 'Do you think you will ever get married?' A flood of relief came over me then. I knew the question was coming from someone who had asked herself the same question many times already. There were other people who had gone through all that doubting too! Nice people! Other young women who had had their self-image as women so severely damaged that they too had wondered if they were entitled to anything life had to offer. My three years with nearly one hundred young women with disabilities began a slow healing process. We laughed and cried together. We experienced illness and even deaths amongst us. But we felt so strong! There I realised how strong women are, especially when we have to fight to overcome something — in our case our disabilities. There I discovered what sharing meant, and accepting people's differences whether they be of colour, class, religion or experience of disability. I began to accept my differences, my uniqueness, as something to be proud of.

When I left that intense community and went back again to join the 'real' world, I felt my battle was just beginning. I wanted a relationship with a man to prove to myself, and the world, that I too was lovable. I believed at that time that the able-bodied world was paradise, and I, an outsider, was constantly knocking on the door asking to be allowed in. Being 'let in' meant sex. When the big event happened after a great deal of manoeuvering by me, I was disappointed to discover that music and shooting stars and little pink hearts did not magically appear. Nor did the gates to heaven open. In fact, on that first occasion, the other person involved turned over, lit a cigarette and said, 'I don't really love you, you know', and I realised then that the key to everlasting joy was not so simple to find.

I cannot pinpoint when I first began to listen to the experiences of able-bodied women and relate them to my own. It may have been when someone said that she couldn't go out of the house because her skin was too spotty, or when a beautiful black woman told me how all her life she had wanted to be white and blotchy like her friend at school, or it could have been when a friend of mine who had always been my envy for being followed around by drooling men, said that she was so lonely because people only reacted to her stunning body, and never to the person inside it. It may have been when my family began to talk about one of its female members who had put on weight and had, in their eyes, become not only unattractive, but somehow outrageously undutiful in her role as an ornament. It may have been none of this that made the turning point for me, but instead it could have been the way some of the women put their arms round me and called me their beautiful sister, that made me begin to see that we are not so different after all. We are all made to feel that our role is firstly to be beautiful in a highly stereotyped way, secondly to be interesting and amusing company to men, and thirdly, good servants. My experience of finding that I was not necessarily any of those things is the experience of most women sooner or later. I have been lucky enough to discover that I am still a whole and worthwhile person and feel that all those dark years linked me profoundly to other women, particularly those who have not only been oppressed for being women, but also have been oppressed for being 'different' and have laid the foundations of a magnificent joint struggle for liberation.

MERRY

Merry, who was born in Kenya, is 30 years old. When she was born her left hip joint was completely missing and the femur was very short. Her family decided to return to England as it was clear she would need a lot of medical attention. Contrary to the doctors' predictions, she was able to walk given a shoe with long metal struts and a rocker on the bottom. At the age of 11 she had to start to wear a full-length caliper, but by then she was already keen on several sports and managed to continue with tennis and swimming. Until she was 14, she attended a school where the teachers had enough sense to let her do what she enjoyed. Unfortunately her family then moved and at the new school things were different. She was never allowed to forget that she had an impairment and was discouraged in many ways from continuing with sport. On leaving school, Merry first trained as a psychologist and then taught for a couple of years so that she could become an educational psychologist. Whilst teaching she found her impairment to be a positive advantage because she taught in a deprived area and many of the young-

sters desperately needed to be needed. Merry says she almost
never did her own shopping or cleaning because there was
always at least one youngster begging to be able to do it.
There were also invariably queues of pupils waiting to carry
her bags and books in school. She went on to work as an
educational psychologist but had increasing back pain and
finally had to stop wearing the caliper after spending months
on her back. Her own specialist recommended an amputation
but it was the doctor to whom she was sent for a second
opinion who worked out that it was the design of the caliper
which had caused the curvature in her spine and the resulting
back pain which is why she has never used the caliper again.
Unfortunately it proved impossible to design a problem-free
caliper, so she has used crutches ever since. Very recently,
however, she has had an operation to give her an artificial
hip-joint and this may help her to walk at least round the
house on the same sort of shoe that she had as a child.
Merry is now completing doctoral research on the effects on
people with impairments of their treatment in society.

My growing awareness of myself as a woman who is physically disabled has come about very gradually and in three
phases that I can identify. Although the phases didn't really
happen separately, it's easier to describe things that way.
First of all, women's liberation entered my world. That
women should have equal choice and do whatever appealed
to them most, seemed obvious to me. I couldn't at the time
see the significance of women 'burning their bras' and I was
annoyed at what seemed to me to be nit-picking about
words . . . all this fuss about 'chair*man*' for example. Slowly,
though, I understood more and more. I came to see how the
system (education, the law, the norms of marriage, medicine
and language, etc.) subtly and not so subtly works to ensure
that women occupy a certain position in society: a dependent and inferior position. I began to understand the power
of the assumption about us and the images of us in papers,
films, etc., to shape our lives. And myself? I saw myself as

quite liberated at first and then, rapidly, very liberated. I stopped plucking my eyebrows, shaving my legs ... and wearing bras! I started insisting that mechanics explain to me whatever I could usefully know about my car. I started being very careful about words, aware now of how they influence our behaviour and thoughts. I fell in love and chose to live with a man who willingly shared house-work, and more, encouraged me in my career and my many activities, including those that kept me from him. The list is longer, but would probably be tedious.

The second phase is about my disablement. Although my leg was deformed from birth, I can't say I was disabled, or handicapped until my teens, when I began to find my activi-ties limited by back pain, caused by the caliper which forced a curve on my spine. Anyway, plenty must have sunk in by then about my status in society, because when, as a sixth-former, I ran a club for people who were disabled, I used to rush about efficiently, trying to appear as different as I possibly could from the club members, and as similar as possible to the able-bodied helpers! Many years later, whilst lying on my back trying to recover from the results of wearing the caliper all those years, I began to think about how much of the language used about us (who are disabled) is negative. Youngsters would look at me and ask, 'What's WRONG with that lady's leg?' and parents (if they didn't shut the child up and rush away guiltily) would reply, 'She's got a BAD leg.' Not, anyway, the most instructive answer! People talk of us as invalids — in-valid! Well no one was ever going to call me that again and get away with it! Slowly I realised what had happened to me; how I had been con-descended to and treated according to people's stereotypes about what I ought to be like; how my leg had so often been politely ignored. I began to see how much energy had to be spent on preventing people from making me look as normal as possible (i.e. as able-bodied as possible). Even more slowly I began to see how, all my life, I had worked hard at being 'well adjusted' and making sure that that was how others saw me. And it started to become clear what that meant. It meant smiling when I was in pain and reassuring whoever I was with. It meant only discussing my leg if I could find something funny to tell about it. It meant accepting whatever the doctors did to me (psychologically as well as physically) with unquestioning courage. All in all it meant being very untrue to myself. (By the way, if you're prepared to take the risk, you can have wonderful fun acting MAL-adjusted, especially if you're with a friend who's also disabled and who is doing the same. Once my friend and I decided to act out the stereotype about not knowing how to act in public. We were eating a meal with a lot of other people and when we saw that some 'hundreds and thousands' — those little bits of coloured sugar — had been spilt on the table, we took our opportunity. We licked our hands very noticeably, squashed them down on the hundreds and thousands and then licked them off agian, laughing and nudging each other. We seemed to laugh away the strain of all those years of trying extra hard to be sure of doing everything right.) Then suddenly the system's role became clear too. I saw that WE are an oppressed group, like people who are black, women and so on; that segregated and substandard education, a physical environment that does not take our needs into account, job discrimination, housing discrimination, lack of aids and services and the threat or actuality of institutionalisation keep us dependent and always ready to please. To justify this treatment, people are taught, through the media for example, to view us in certain rigid and negative ways — as stupid, unable to look after ourselves, uninterested in the world and so on, and so on.

This helped me to understand more about my behaviour, by seeing how I'd taken in so many of these oppressive ideas and values. I'd behaved the way I did in the club because I had learnt to look down on other people who were disabled unless they too acted 'normally'. Even more, I was scared of being categorised like them and therefore treated like them, by the able-bodied. I had this strange desire for respect! Somehow, at least a little of my humanness remained intact in relation to others who are disabled because I made firm friends with another woman who was visibly disabled, who helped run the same club. Somehow, deep down, I'm sure we always know what's right. Anyway, now I laugh when I remember how I used to walk faster if I saw another person on crutches, trying to prove I wasn't as feeble as they were! That's the in-group competitiveness that oppression breeds, just like women trying to be more attractive than the others.

That, in a way, brings me on to the third phase, where my understanding of the oppression of women and the oppression of those who are disabled comes together. Well, I kept asking myself, 'What is it about me that permitted me to understand about women's liberation and *act* on it so quickly?' The answer wasn't long in coming. It has been rare in my life that my femininity has been acknowledged by girls or boys, women or men. I went to ordinary schools and my school friends (with a thankful exception of one) did not see me as part of the teenage scene, or as a competitor for boyfriends. When I went out with my first ever, very good-looking boyfriend, school friends were openly amazed that *I* had been able to capture such a creature. I was not seen to be a woman, so I did not really see myself as a woman. Stopping all attempts to look like a pin-up was therefore easy — I had nothing to lose and everything to gain. Increasingly my long-buried feelings of differentness have come up. When I listened to, or read about, other women growing up as women, I felt a numbness which said 'What are they talking about? and 'Where was I?' It's not that I'm saying I hadn't tried to look 'pretty', for instance, and even thought that I looked pretty sometimes. It's just that the implications of that were different for me. The phrase 'Never mind about your leg, dear, at least you've got a pretty face' rings loud and clear in my head. My prettiness was not about being feminine, for them. It was a let-out; it redeemed me from being just a freak in their eyes and permitted them to normalise me in their minds. It has been rare in my life that I have feared men getting sexual with me, because most men don't see me as a sex object in the same way as they see most women. For THAT I am profoundly grateful!!! . . . But if only more women had made me feel like a woman. . . . Besides all this, I began to see the extra-heavy push to dependency that women who are disabled experience, and the costs (not forgetting the benefits) of fighting against that (psychological, physical *and* financial costs). It's hard to hang on to your good feelings about yourself when you're being accused of being unrealistic, too independent, overcompensating, etc., etc. On the other hand, it's true that the rewards are enormous, and it's good to know that there are others also determined to get things right.

So where am I now? Well I'm in all sorts of exciting and tingly places. For a start I'm doing what I can to change the system that relegated us to dependency. To that end I've joined the Liberation Network of People with Disabilities. We've still got a lot to learn, but we've already got a lot to offer and a lot to teach. Over the last few months I've made lots of close friends with people who are disabled and know a friendship with them quite unlike my friendships with the able-bodied. Some of the other women who've written pieces for this book are people I love dearly and share with so much. We understand a great deal without need for words. We can be human with each other about things that the able-bodied are usually too impatient to wait for or too bound up in only one way of experiencing things to appreciate. We laugh helplessly together, cry together and are highly committed to each other. We know that when we are fighting to get things right for everyone in our oppressed group, we are fighting for each other, and when we are fighting for each other, we are fighting for everyone. We know we have a whole lot of treasures to offer to the world and are happy to know that we still have a lot to learn. And about myself as a women, particularly? Recently I ventured to tell a woman friend that I felt I wanted to call her my sister (the first time ever) and wept long and loud with her. And she just loved me.

Note: I feel a need to add a little about words. A short while ago, a member of the Union of the Physically Impaired against Segregation pointed out to me that the phrase 'people with disabilities' makes our lack of abilities sound like an inevitable result of our physical condition, whereas it is usually the result of society failing to provide us with the necessary aids, etc. Society actually does have both the necessary technology and financial resources to enable us to live independently, if it chose to allocate its resources in this way. To refer to the actual physical condition, the Union speaks of the physically impaired, and to refer to the results of society's attitudes towards us, they refer to disablement. Thus when they say a person is disabled, they mean disabled by society. Unfortunately lots of my friends react unfavourably to the word 'impaired' and also say that it's not much good using the word disabled to mean something quite different from what everyone else means unless you say so each time. So there is a bit of a search going on for good, perhaps quite new, words.

MAGGIE

Maggie, who is 31 years old, is severely deaf and wears a hearing-aid. She is a single parent with two daughters aged 7 and 3. Maggie works part-time as a teacher of drama to deaf students in further education. A feminist, who is politically active in the disability world, she is studying for a degree in psychology at the Open University. Her other interests are performing mime and growing vegetables.

I started to go deaf fifteen years ago. In the beginning my hearing loss was slight but looking back it seems as if the feeling of disability was far greater then than now, for it seemed to permeate my whole being. At eighteen, I was a lively, extrovert, intelligent and attractive drama student with very definite ideas about my future life plan which centred largely on a career in the theatre. I found I missed bits of conversation sometimes in noisy situations but this happened so infrequently that I attributed it to lapses in concentration and the Glaswegian accents around me. Little threatening thoughts that I might be inheriting the family deafness were dismissed until the college began to notice my difficulty and I was sent to an ear, nose and throat specialist. He diagnosed hereditary, incurable, progressive nerve deafness and said that I would probably be profoundly deaf in about five years' time. My first feelings were ones of enormous guilt at having 'let my parents down' and I kept the news secret until the college wrote to them. But the guilt of being less than a perfect person remained and grew, as my deafness progressed.

I readjusted my life plan as one who has been told she has five years left to live. I found I could bluff my way out of awkward situations by acting the part of a rather scatty dolly bird. It wasn't that I couldn't hear you but rather that I was such a feather-brained, aspiring actress that I just didn't understand what you meant. It seemed more acceptable to be a 'normal' silly butterfly than an intelligent deaf woman. In this role I made no demands on anyone but I experienced a different kind of oppression which led me to my first awareness of sexism and the oppression of women in general.

When I thought about a future when I would be profoundly deaf I shuddered with horror. I wouldn't be able to act because I would lose control of my voice. All my present voice training would be wasted. I wouldn't be able to work at anything other than cleaning or assembly line work. I would have to give up my present social life and take up interests where I didn't have to mix with people. I could, of course, get married and take the easy way out of the employment problem. If I were a wife and mother I wouldn't lose my self-respect as it is fine for mothers to stay at home. But would any man want a deaf woman for a wife? Since my deafness was hereditary would I want to watch children of mine go through all this trauma? Would I wish a miserable deaf woman on any child for a mother? Whichever way I turned to think, the negative answer that I was deaf seemed to destroy any shred of hope. I can only think that I learned to expect so little from my future because I had somehow soaked up these prevailing attitudes towards women with disabilities as a hearing woman and taken them over to crush myself in my own deafness.

Five years later, I was married to a life-long friend and working as a teacher of drama in a comprehensive school. The frivolous butterfly had long since vanished into oblivion. I could still hear, with the help of an expensive hearing-aid, and could communicate with my husband and friends quite easily in one-to-one situations. In groups, such as the staff-room at school or gatherings in my own home, however, I was lost, since, by now, I had to see the speaker's face to lipread as well as hear. People's heads toss and turn, mouths are covered by hands, so many consonants look alike on the lips and by the time you have translated one difficult word the next sentence has passed by unnoticed. I discovered that neither hearing-aids nor lipreading were the miracle solutions they were cracked up to be. Being a woman made things 'easy' once again. I smiled and nodded my way through hour after hour, looked good and cooked nice food. In those days it seemed acceptable for the men to do all the talking and the woman to listen and play the part of passive admiring wives. My armchair interest in the growing women's movement told me otherwise but I coudn't see any way out. I could still ape 'normality' but the woman inside was in despair.

My ENT specialist told me not to worry. I would eventually come to terms with the change in my life. He gave me no indication as to how I was to come to terms with a world viewed largely through a plate glass window where other people live, laugh and suffer and barely know of my existence. Deprived of much positive feedback on the woman I really was, my self-esteem took an insidious dive. I began to mistrust my own perception of the world and the people around me. How could I be sure of my impressions when I couldn't hear? When the views of others differed I quickly adjusted mine. They were right because they could hear and my experience seemed invalid. I felt I had little to offer anyone and rather than face rejection, I avoided people. Grieving over the lively, gregarious woman I had once been, I felt very isolated.

I seemed to be near breaking point when one evening something happened that proved to be the beginnings of my birth as a deaf woman. I was in an Indian restaurant with friends doing my little smiling and nodding act when I noticed the people opposite. At first, I thought they were drama students because they were so lively and expressive but then I noticed the sign language. They were deaf like me! They were happy! They were laughing and talking and didn't give a damn that the whole place knew they were deaf. I stared and stared with fascination and found I could follow more of their conversation than I could the talk at my own table even though I couldn't follow the signs. My years of pretence seemed suddenly absurd. I had been making things 'normal' and easy for everyone except myself. I was a deaf woman. It was time to give up my mourning and come out deaf.

We had been on the list of an adoption society for several months but as my first positive thoughts about my disability began to take hold I realised that I had been allowing my deafness to deprive us of so much. This body had a right to carry a baby and give birth. In saying our children shouldn't be born I was saying implicitly that I shouldn't have been born. OK so maybe our children could go deaf but with me as a mother they would have the finest possible expert to help them. Even if they didn't go deaf they were going to have a magnificent deaf mother. Not for our children the passive smiling noddy or the pretty cook. They were going to grow up seeing deaf people treated with respect. It became my most important goal not only for my children but for myself and all deaf people.

Whilst I was expecting my first child I met some women who had been born deaf who introduced me to the most revolutionary hearing-aid ever invented — sign language. Lipreading the clearest speaker is fine for half an hour but after that my eyes water and my brain becomes confused and I am no longer alert enough to continue. No relationship can be made or continued in half-hour stretches but if people can fingerspell or sign I can enjoy their company into the early hours of the morning without strain. It takes ten minutes to learn the fingerspelling alphabet and when people fingerspell the first letters of words I can lip-read them with ease. I find that, once fingerspelling has been mastered and a relationship established, people are more motivated to learn how to sign. There is something very special about communicating with deaf people which can terrify you or enthrall you depending on what kind of person you are. We look at each other when we talk and this looking plus more explicit non-verbal communication involves a high level of self-disclosure which is not normally present in spoken conversation where people hardly look at each other at all. Words can lie and cover up but the face and body rarely do. My special needs demand your honesty and glimpses of your preciously guarded inner self. 'I'm sorry, don't worry, never mind, dear', you say when I tell you I am deaf. But it is your face that reads 'fear' not mine. And it is your fear of my deafness I have to help you with when we first meet. Sometimes I fail and the pain of your rejection goes down to join the pain of a thousand rejections. When I succeed, I am Maggie, lively, intelligent and lovable. As a mother of two small children I can be excluded in subtle ways even by those who otherwise understand my needs. People will speak beautifully for me and then drop the signs and turn to talk 'normally' to the children. What are they saying? Is it trivial or important? Don't I exist any more? A child can be rushed from the room for a wee wee or a drink and I am left wondering what calamity has occurred. Ears have heard what my eyes were not allowed to see. Doctors and school-teachers address questions to the children which would otherwise be addressed to me. Hey, I'm their mother! What is it that isn't fit for my ears? I can't let such small things pass without comment, since my children are learning that it is easier to get what you want from people who can hear and too much effort to bother people who are deaf and who are not important anyway.

A recent visitor laughingly remarked, 'Your children speak to people as if everyone were deaf.' Yes, they do when I am there because they acknowledge my right to be included — my right to exist. Even when I am one deaf woman among a hundred who can hear it is still my right. When I walk into the busy staffroom at college or join a room full of friends and see them switch, as if by reflex action, to speaking and signing so that I can understand, I feel a glow of joy. This is how it should be because I am important and lovable enough to be included and when I am included I am no longer disabled.

BARBARA

Barbara, who is 31 years old, went up to Oxford in 1968, where she read English Language and Literature at St Hilda's College. She met her husband, Roland, who was also a student, and they married in Oxford in 1970. In 1971 she gained a first-class honours degree in English and began teaching at Berkhamsted School for Girls in 1972. Later that year she had a car accident, swerving to avoid a dog,

and broke her back. For a year she was confined to a wheelchair but now walks with a stick. She can only manage
limited distances very slowly and tires easily. In 1974 she
gave birth to a son, Dominic, and in 1978 a daughter,
Corrina. Currently she is a tutor for Wolsey Hall
Correspondence College, working at home.

> One minute I held the tiller,
> The next, the rudder's snapped;
> A split second, and life's changed course.

Thus wrote Mrs K. Thomas, who was a nursing auxiliary at
Stoke Mandeville when I was a patient, in a sensitive poem
recording the impressions patients had given her of their
reactions to disability. This sense of numbed shock, of
powerlessness, anxiety and loss of direction, was my first
reasoned response when the realisation that I was partially
paralysed penetrated my brain. Initially, I had felt thankful
to be alive — I had had a very serious head injury at the
same time as I fractured my spine and was not expected to
survive. However, this mood of unquestioning gratitude
collapsed as I found myself forced to consider what quality
of life was left to me. Anger — a feeling that my body was
now flawed, no longer as God meant it to be — and frustration
succeeded. I hadn't been *made* like this, why should I be
expected to live like it?

This destruction of my self-confidence was the most
significant and far-reaching effect my paraplegia had on me.
I felt that I was no longer acceptable, let alone desirable.
All around me in the ward, marriages and long-standing
relationships were dissolving under the strain imposed by the
woman's disability. Out of ten or twelve young women in
the ward with me, of whom nine were married or engaged,
mine was the only relationship that eventually survived,
although only three or four actually broke up while the wife
was in hospital. A marriage was not *expected* to hold together; one of the staff said to me, 'You're married, aren't

you? Well, that won't last!' Indeed, I felt so imperfect and inadequate that it seemed positively selfish to expect my husband to remain with what I had become, so I tried to persuade him to divorce me. Fortunately, though bitterly hurt by my suggestion, he refused. Why is it that so many marriages, especially of younger women who become disabled, break up? Part of the reason may be that many men find the role of nurse and carer suddenly imposed on them by the exigencies of their wife's condition totally unacceptable, it often being necessary to help in emptying bladder and bowel and in changing incontinence pads and even tampons. To a woman much of this is more or less instinctive — we quickly learn to cope with a baby's nappies. The determining factor is perhaps the nature of the relationship, although the attitude of professionals and people around to one's disability is important, too. Young couples have had less time to form a bond, have accumulated less joint memories, and perhaps less joint responsibilities, in the shape of children and mortgages. If a relationship has been one where physical considerations are of the greatest importance, where shared interests centre solely around dancing and sport, and where the female's role is primarily to enhance the male's status amongst his peers, then obviously the disablement of the woman is going to provoke a crisis. (The only physical interests my husband and I shared were punting and midnight walks along the tow-path — which we'd had to forgo on leaving Oxford, anyway!) The attitude of the two partners before and after disability to each other and to themselves is crucial, and that is why a damaged self-image can have such an impact. It took me a long time to stop (mentally) apologising to my husband for existing, and to stop regarding him, as others around me did, as something of a saint because he did *not* leave me.

One's self-confidence is subjected to much unintentional battering by the public at large, too. Suddenly, one discovers that one is imbecilic ('does you wife take sugar?') and quite possibly unemployable. I had been a teacher of

English at a private girls' school in Berkhamsted, Hertford-shire for five weeks when I broke my back in 1972. I was shattered when they asked me to resign because it was going to prove too difficult to arrange for me to teach in one room on the ground floor as opposed to moving from class to class in the usual way. I felt totally rejected, not only was my body impaired, but it seemed that even my mind was no longer of any use. Another problem a newly disabled woman may well have to find a solution to is that of the over-protectiveness of her family and friends. Being treated (albeit with the best of intentions) as a helpless invalid, discourages independence, and can be very damaging to one's self-esteem. I also discovered that a disability renders one neuter. Disabled people are not supposed to retain the feelings and instincts of the able-bodied, and this is an attitude one encounters among the caring professions in hospitals looking after the newly disabled, when a person is most vulnerable. In a mixed spinal ward at Stoke Mandeville Hospital it is at the moment (I'm trying to change it!) con-sidered quite acceptable, if not ideal, for male and female patients to use the same lavatories and bathrooms with only curtains, not doors, to screen them from each other. They are thus expected to perform intimate bodily functions with very little privacy, a situation that most able-bodied people would find quite intolerable.

The sexual problems facing the disabled have thankfully received much attention in the last few years. When I broke my back, the hospital gave me no help or advice at all. The nearest to counselling I received were a few coarse jokes and innuendoes which, though admittedly amusing, were not of much practical value. The women's sexual role is supposedly largely passive, and while I appreciate that the impact of sudden impotence on a young man, whose conception of himself is rooted in his virility, can be devastating, I think this supposed passivity of the female explains the lack of support and help most disabled women receive. The profes-sionals simply did not realise the importance of sexuality to the restoration of one's self-esteem. It was not until some three years after my injury, when I had been seeing an eminent gynaecologist and sexologist, Mr Desmond Bluett, for some time on a private basis, and had been receiving from him the advice, practical help, and counselling not available at the hospital, that I began to function again as a sexual being. Mr Bluett understood the importance of this to me; until I could respond to my husband, I felt that I was no longer contributing anything to our relationship — my sexual failure had become a symbol of all my other imagined inadequacies. The rediscovery of my own sexuality restored my sense of identity, and my self-respect. It was nearly the most important factor in my rehabilitation.

Putting oneself together again mentally after disability (which will serve as my definition of what rehabilitation involves) is obviously vital. Bitterness and self-pity can wreck a person, and of course can ruin a marriage. So can constant self-abasement, because people tend to take one on one's own valuation. So if a woman is convinced that she is worthless and merits only a kind of condescending pity, then that is how she will be regarded. Two other subsidiary factors helped *me* to regain my self-confidence and so indirectly maintained the stability of my marriage. The first was the support and help of my entire family, especially my beloved father, and which one of my brothers translated into practical terms by finding me a job as a tutor with a correspondence college. This demonstrated to me that at least mentally I still functioned adequately. The second was the birth of my two children, the eldest, Dominic, within two years of my injury, and the baby, Corrina, some four years later. Despite some bladder and bowel complications caused by a particularly difficult first labour and delivery in a local hospital (which Mr Bluett, who delivered Corrina by Caesarean section, has only just after nearly six years, put right, since he alone appreciated that the problems I was experiencing were not spinal but gynaecological, resulting from the damage to my pelvic floor muscles in childbirth)

I discovered that pregnancy and children themselves are a wonderful morale-booster. At last my body was acting as a female body was supposed to — I felt blessedly *normal* while pregnant, and doctors were interested not in my back, which I'd had enough of by then, but in my developing baby. Once my children were born, I became almost immediately the centre of their lives, whose presence was rewarded by smiles and whose absence or anger provoked cries of distress. It was wonderful to feel so *necessary!*

Most important of all was the attitude of my husband, Roland. He instinctively struck the perfect balance between helping me, and allowing me to do things for myself to regain my independence. One example will suffice. Roland would never help me to stand up — in any case, unsolicited aid upsets my equilibrium, which is never very stable — but if I fell, he was always there either to catch me or to pick me up. To the uninitiated outsider, it must often have seemed that he was being heartless and cruel to leave me struggling to manage running our home as best I could crawling around on my knees. (Until I had an operation on my hip, I couldn't walk even with crutches, and it was impossible to get the enormous wheelchair the hospital supplied through the front door of our tiny cottage, quite apart from the lack of any space to manoeuvre it once it was inside.) Roland's attitude incited me to prove that I could still perform normal domestic duties, albeit slowly and clumsily. He showed a complete acceptance of the limitations and implications of my medical condition, coupled with a constructive sympathy to help me to come to terms with it. Because he made it clear to me that in all but the most basic physical sense I was still the same girl he married, I began to look on myself in that way, too.

This whole consideration of the psychological effects of disability on me raises the further question of whether my experiences were typical; whether in fact there are special problems attached to being a disabled *woman*. The crucial element seems to me to be not the *sex* of the disabled person, but his or her attitude. The greatest problem for a woman with a disability would seem to be that she may feel that she is no longer sexually attractive or lovable; her self-confidence, which is strongly linked to her conception of the image she wishes to project of herself and which represents how she intends society to regard her, is seriously shaken. She feels ugly, faulty, impaired and worthless. In my case, once my self-image was restored, I ceased to feel mentally crippled. Indeed, most of the friends I have made since my disability have to make a conscious effort to remember that I am physically handicapped — it is a peripheral facet of me they frequently overlook, not something of central importance. Until a disabled woman learns, as I did, to place a higher value on herself and realises that to many men she is still personally attractive, she will indeed be doubly disadvantaged.

SUE

Sue, who is in her 30s, lives in an isolated village in Kent with Ian and her small son. She is taking a degree course in sociology at the University of Kent. She is a radical feminist and 'a very private person'.

When I woke up the morning of 1 June 1976, a normal day, I did not know it was to be the beginning of the end. The end of freedom, spontaneity, social anonymity; the beginning of fear, pain, existential isolation; the ambiguity of social ostracism/public property. I did not know it on that June morning but I was to become THE DISABLED; the beginning of the frightening descent into the world of the 'social minority'.

MS came suddenly, dream-like. On my usual walk down the lane which marks my country home, legs became heavy, the unconscious movement became conscious. I fell among

the grasses and wild flowers, no real alarm yet, wondering.
The strange consciousness of movement receded, I continued,
but days later it reappeared. I went to the doctor. 'Er,
Doctor, I-um-don't seem to be able to walk properly' —
embarrassed, conscious of sounding silly. He eyed me bleakly
and handed me some tranquillisers. I went home and threw
them away. Symptoms continued and varied. I visited the
medical profession again. This time he was not amused —
look Mrs Housewife you are depressed/isolated/neurotic/
female. Are you taking the pills? No? Exasperated, take
these pills. I take the pills, symptoms persist. I go back
to the overworked doctor. Repeat my story. He tries psychological approach (after all, he's on duty at the local 'mental
hospital' sometimes, he has an interest in psychology). 'Do
you find walking easier when you are not with your husband?' 'No.' I am not being helpful. 'Do you find it more
difficult out of doors?'. 'Yet — I keep feeling like I'm going
to fall over (and there's no furniture to hang on to).' Ah
hah — his face brightens up, he's got it — agoraphobia. I'm
not at all convinced, I ask for an examination. Smile fades,
he refuses, says its not necessary — I am agoraphobic. I don't
feel any better, but I have a label. I go home and report
that I am an agoraphobic. There follow months when I nearly
kill myself, forcing painful legs on long walks, bike rides,
in an effort to de-agoraphobic myself, combined with ama-
teur psychiatry nights of 'where did I go wrong'. I couldn't
get the feel of being an agoraphobic. I go back to the doctor;
this time he's had enough. I am a hypochondriac — heated
words — the patient answers back. I'm shown hastily out of
the surgery shouting, 'Next time I see you I'll be in a bloody
wheelchair.' Prophetic words. The next day I collapse, an
embarrassed doctor (but covering up well with professional
ethos) orders an ambulance.

I am in hospital. Hospital, where people go to get better,
doctors in white coats are gods of medical science and technology, patients are models of gratitude, subservience and
stiff in the upper lip and everybody is happy. Ladies in nice

nighties, smiling, pretty flowers surrounding the bed of pain. Men in white coats who stand at the end of those beds don't actually speak to the case in the bed, don't actually look at the case in the bed, especially if you have something nasty they can't bring themselves to tell you about. I'm transferred to another hospital. I prefer this place — at least it's more honest for my type of patient — no more pretence that everything is all right. No more ladies in nice nighties, no more sweetness and light; the hopeless cases. An old workhouse, institutional green with pipes running down the walls. The staff leave you alone, no more forced gaiety and 'interest'. I remember facing one young doctor saying, 'I've got MS, haven't I?' (I still don't know where that idea came from as I had no real idea what those words meant.) He, looking embarrassed and surprised said, 'Yes.' Then I said, 'That's curable isn't it?' 'No', he said, 'It's incurable.' These gods in white coats, whom as a child you always knew would make you better, who could make test-tube babies, transplant hearts, kidneys, could not help me. I was incurable; one of the hopeless ones. But that young doctor could not face telling me I was one of the hopeless so he said I would get better, I was the type of case who never, but never, had another attack. I was reprieved, saved, and until I started reading about the disease I was now bound up with, I believed him (almost).

The day started at 6 o'clock with a nice cup of tea, but not for me. As I had just managed to sleep a few hours previously and had nothing to do all day except lie in bed, the prospect of being awake was not appealing. They gave up on me, merely muttering angrily and rattling the tea trolley. Not so fortunate were the older residents, who were got out of bed and sat in a chair for the next 13 interminable hours. Woe are those who are powerless, helpless and helped. An older woman who had one of the most beautiful and dignified faces I have seen, sat immobile in her chair day after day, refusing to be alive to what was happening to her, except when her husband came at night and loved her, and she became human again. Porridge time came around one morning and in bustled one of those guardian angels, a nurse. 'Come on dear,' said the 20-year-old to the 70-year-old, 'Eat up your nice porridge.' The woman sat unspeaking while the nurse tried to push the spoon into the unwilling mouth. The ward was quiet, the helpless looked away while the helper forced in the porridge. The woman turned her head, wordlessly, tears streaming down her face. The nurse, momentarily defeated, angrily turned to the helpless for support, 'She's got to eat it, it's good for her.' Man's inhumanity to man. But then when you are the helpless, dignity is a luxury you cannot afford.

I finally left that place of hidden pain and despair and got back into the mainstream of life — but with a difference, I was now 'disabled'. I was entering the world of 'normal' and 'abnormal' and I was soon to find that I was firmly on the side of the 'abnormal' divide. It's a strange and frightening experience to leave hospital 'different' from when you went in. I somehow expected the world to have changed because my experience of it had, but it was just the same, it was I who had changed. Hospital was horrible, but at least you had a place in it, everybody was ill, but out there you were on your own. Life somehow became relegated in the mind as 'then' and 'now'. The splutter of interest I had received on my initial going into hospital, interest in my diagnosis from the medics, 'hope you get better soon' from friends, quickly dissipated. The medical profession figuratively pulled down the blinds on my case, told me it was all a matter of attitude and departed, and friends, ah yes, friends, I didn't find I had any, not at least so as I would notice.

I was confused, I still felt fundamentally the same. My body was different, I knew that all right, but inside it was me. Normality after all is what you know. The male who is very short is normal to himself, it is other people who make him aware of an 'abnormality'. The 'ugly' female is 'normal' to herself (try denying your own being), it's the others who make her 'abnormal'. After all if we were all very short and ugly (decide for yourself what that means) a person unlike that would be 'abnormal'. 'Normality' and 'abnormality' are socially defined. It also has to be a relative concept, we are all normal/abnormal to the social norm, in varying degrees. Disability can and sometimes does interfere with the practical running of a life, but it is the reaction and non-action of society which causes disablement. There is no such thing as THE DISABLED, there are just people. On leaving hospital and finding the mantle of 'disabled' placed firmly upon my unwilling shoulders I entered a world which was alien, absurd and ultimately defeating. My weak grasp on my identity was no real match for the massed forces of society who firmly believed themselves as 'normal' and myself just as firmly as 'abnormal'. I found myself inhabiting a stereotype. I became my illness, I was of interest only because of it. And as a person in a wheelchair I illicited embarrassment, avoidance, condescension, personal questions. With a growing sense of unreality, I noticed people were not talking to me, only to the person who was standing on their own two feet behind, and if they did they were inexplicably embarrassed, or talking loudly. I became public property, anyone could come up to me (being friendly of course) and ask me 'What's happened to you dear?' and they all seemed to know somebody or somebody who knew somebody who had MS and then proceeded to tell me in graphic detail what happened to them.

Friends either departed or tried manfully to ignore what had happened to me. I was surrounded by a conspiracy of silence. I discovered the topic I wanted and needed to discuss was taboo. Talk about broken affairs, politics, etc., was OK, in fact socially desirable, but my fear and pain of my experience was not. Such attention as I received was jocularity and curiosity from the insensitive (of which I found many) and embarrassment from the more sensitive. When I did mention the bewilderment I felt at the treatment I was now experiencing I was told, 'They are embarrassed, they cannot cope.'

So I had become an embarrassment! They cannot cope, but they don't have to, I felt like screaming, I have to and they are making it impossible. I discovered the 'sick role'. The 'sick role' is society's niche for THE DISABLED. You must behave as 'the sick' at all times but never complain about it. You must allow your person to have good works vented upon it, it makes THEM feel better, accept with a gracious smile the fuss, offers of 'help' you don't need. It puts you in the 'sick role' the good feel good, everyone is happy. 'They are just trying to help' — but whom they are actually helping is supposition in need of analysis that these good souls would never attempt.

Going out became a nightmare, I was public property. People either staring intently into my face, or quickly looking away. I have been told by friends that the notice I cause is due to the disparate images I present — 'I'm young and attractive, I don't present the "disabled" image expected' (you work out the implications of that one). Places I had taken for granted became inaccessible to me, cinemas, restaurants, many shops, people's houses, etc. We devised unorthodox methods for combating society's thoughtlessness (and subconscious efforts?) to exclude me, I went piggy-back (feminism gone wild!). In need of some light relief we decided to storm *The Life of Brian* — it's amazing when you think about it that people who logically need cheering up and entertainment are the very people who are most often denied it. (Cinema modern, many, many steps, no lift.) We managed to get in at a slack time, and after the film, sat in our seats like a couple of fugitives, hearts beating, waiting to make a break. Now — it would be quiet — made our way to the foyer only to be confronted by a huge queue, mouths agape, who watched our every movement into the chair, which had been carefully hidden away in a cupboard as an unusual object. Implicit in the crowd's behaviour — what's a person like you doing in a place of enjoyment? Moral tale: Know your place — but then I always have had trouble with that one.

So, I wheel through this wonderland which for me, by accident, has become a nightmare, a living embarrassment. I'm told I'm lucky, Ian is told how wonderful he is, I am told how wonderful he is and how lucky I am. It's great for the self-esteem (it's a well-known sociological/psychological fact that we 'disabled' have low self-esteem). Implicit implication; he's wonderful/a saint for staying with an undesirable property like you. You (disabled) are lucky not to be alone, unwanted in an institution. No one has ever said he is lucky (unthinkable), or he obviously stays with you because you give as much as you take. But then of course, that's an unthinkable proposition, isn't it? After all I'm only one of THE DISABLED.

PS. I realise that a lot of what I have said will be unpopular, or that I can be dismissed as bitter and twisted. Dismiss me if you will, as society has dismissed the feelings and protests of blacks, Jews, gays, women for centuries. Historically it has been proven that powerless groups are not given recognition until they demand and fight for it. Likewise I am not asking for my rights and humanity to be given a place in this society, which like it or not, I belong to — I demand it.

PAT

Pat, who is in her early 30s, contracted polio at 2 years of age which left her paralysed from the waist downwards. She walked with the aid of calipers and crutches until recently but is now confined to a wheelchair due to spinal difficulties. She worked as a secretary for a number of years with the Civil Service until she obtained a place at college and later university. After university, Pat worked for the Royal Free Hospital as Co-ordinator for a Research Project in diseases of the heart, as a secretary for the National Bureau for Handi-

capped Students and currently full-time Advisory and Information Officer for the Disablement Income Group, where she
advises on the financial problems of, and for, disabled people.
She was awarded a Winston Churchill Travelling Scholarship
(1980) to study self-help housing schemes in Alberta,
Canada, for mentally and physically handicapped people.
She is on the Management Committee of the Crossroads
Care Attendent Scheme and Chairperson and Founder of
the Islington Disablement Sports Association.

'Your mummy has gone to heaven', said my aunt and with
that phrase I knew I had become an orphan. My father had
died shortly after I had contracted polio when I was two. I
was ten and my brother fourteen years old. Family life had
thus ended when mother went to 'heaven'. When she died,
we had been living in Essex and, being disabled, I attended
the local mixed school for mildly handicapped children.
My brother went to a boarding school in Suffolk. Attending
different schools, in different areas, meant we came under
the care of two different education authorities and this fact
changed the pattern of our lives. It meant we went into the
care of two different authorities with different ideas on how
their charges ought to be cared for. My brother was fostered
with one set of relations during school holidays, whilst I
was to be shared between two families. I was whisked away
to a special boarding school for both mentally and physically
handicapped girls. Rather than catering to the particular
needs of each disability, the school was more of a dumping
ground for society's outcasts. As far as the school was concerned, the common denominator was disability. The fight
for survival as an individual was on.

Being females, we were not, unless very bright, expected
to amount to very much and the level of teaching was to the
lowest and slowest of the class's mentally handicapped. For
example, I was a particularly good reader. Reading lessons
consisted not of individuals reading aloud or to oneself
but a clock-wise session of each individual, whatever level

of reading ability, struggling to read a passage. I used to carry on at my own pace and ignore or forget where the last one had fumbled to. Consequently, I became a target for 'not paying attention' and not finding my place in a book. I had often read it more than twice by the time the class finished it and had lost interest. Taking parts when reading a play proved disastrous and pathetic, as there was no semblance of continuity or cohesiveness. For 'O' levels, the teachers had to tutor the four of us by postal course. It was dull and uninteresting and no one had time to explain 'homework' — whatever that was. Their expectations for our future were either continuing in residential care or being a seamstress. At all costs it was essential that we learn to appreciate a Victorian view of being a woman, sit passively listening to classical music, if possible learn to play a musical instrument, be able to sew the most intricate things and have courteous manners. The norm was passively to obey, at all costs, one's elders. The rebel in me was thus born and forged. I resolved that I was not going to become a seamstress or a 'cripple' in a home. I was going to shape my future or die in the attempt. As I went through my teens I found I was not expected to have adolescent feelings of sexuality or wish to wear pretty things. A disabled woman was a neutered sexual being and a dependent on society and always to be 'grateful' for what was meted out. The burden of passive oppression was crushing. For example, a small thing that incensed me. Every time visitors, particularly the governors, came to the school, we had to remove the awful pinnies that we had to wear at all times, brush our shoes and be ready for inspection and 'answer up' to questions anyone might ask. I was nearly expelled when I smuggled the pinnies back into the class and made everyone put them on just as the governors came into the classroom. The pinnies never fitted and were always marked with slops by those who had difficulty with eating, and by the general debris of the week. It was a shock-horror situation and when asked to explain my actions I tried to explain what it was like to be viewed in a cage, be talked about as if deaf and that people ought to see us how we really were — pathetic creatures shut away in a cupboard of society. One became valueless without shape or form. Every year the RAF held Christmas parties where everyone was treated as an idiot child. Once, when I was thirteen years old, I chose a cuddly toy off the present list and the man who gave it came up to me and started talking to me as if I was four years old. I told him to 'sod off' and was marked as an ungrateful being.

In my school holidays I was beginning to realise that I was not individualistic and self-assertive as I thought and that I had no choice about my life style. The education authorities only allowed school uniforms at all times. My friends at home wore pretty things and were gradually having ideas for their future. My future loomed before me as a struggle to shed the bonds of anonymity. My brother was taking his 'A' levels and laying the foundations of a successful career. Our single reunion every school holiday showed me he spoke well, had a sense of dress and knew where he was going. I felt ashamed. He would tutor me, on his visit, through a book on how to pronounce words and spelling. The school was asked to give me particular attention in these areas but after one or two lessons, it was decided that it was unnecessary! I was expected to do nothing and fulfilled their expectations but with a burning desire to prove everyone wrong. My brother was expected to do well and he did and eventually slipped into his university place.

As a young girl, I was keen to wear fashionable clothes but the two visual images of womanhood were denied me: that of bodily beauty and a sense of fashion. I was plump and as I rarely had any clothes and only those decreed to be 'practical' I did not develop any dress sense. In fact I can remember the two dresses, two jumpers and the three blouses I had. Society quietly decreed that I need not bother to become a 'woman'; my disability precluded such a luxury. But what was worse, it placed me, as I developed, into the

Catch 22 syndrome. That is, I could not choose to opt out
of a sexist role — if I did my choice was not recognised as
a positive decision but just part of being 'disabled' and
therefore my style of dress was not important. Consequently,
the silent pressure by society towards my non-sexuality
forced me to take a sexist role in order to demonstrate my
womanhood; in fact I needed to be ultra-feminine to appear
'normal'.

When I left boarding school at fifteen I went to live
permanently with one family and attended the local ordinary
school, where I flourished and became a studious pupil.
The contrast was so very different. I was expected to study
hard, take exams, complete homework and participate in all
school activities. Although I could not actively join in with
gym, I was expected to attend and sit on the side-lines catch-
ing up on homework. This was a delight to my school chums
who used it as an excuse to 'keep Pat company' but the gym
mistress soon caught on! Outings to factories were part of
the school curriculum and in my class I became the focus
of a threatening classroom strike. The class were off to visit
a paper mill but when informed that I was not going because it would be too tiring for me, the class decided none of
them would go. No one had asked me and the class decided
I ought to choose for myself. Naturally I wanted to go and
eventually, we all went and had an enjoyable day!

As I was still in the care of the education authority it was
decided that I should play the other strong female role, that
of being a secretary. As I was fairly bright it was felt that the
future was a good one. Unfortunately, I had no intention
of becoming one and the thought of spending my days in
an office gave me claustrophobia. It was decided to send me
to a secretarial training college. The college specialised in
retraining for those who had sustained mild industrial injuries,
consequently the emphasis was on hard work and high
job expectation. I underwent the course and it did prove
useful over the years but college also taught me other things.
I was already 'courting' and as female students were in

great demand, I realised sexuality was a viable commodity for companionship and good fun. Also, I learnt that I was expected to hold down a job and look after myself. At 17 years the education authorities decline responsibility for their charges and leave you to fend for yourself to find a home and a job. Although it had always been considered that I needed special care and attention because I was disabled, once I had reached the age barrier all responsibility for my 'special' needs ended. I found a job and living quarters in London where I repeatedly tried to break from the secretarial mould. I was too late to gain further education, I was told, unless I persisted at evening classes. My social life was so full of sports and people that I had little time to study at night. As I had had a poor education, I really did not know how to study or write an essay. Eventually I learnt that there was a women's college where one could study without 'O' or 'A' levels. I applied and was accepted. During the course, I developed a burning desire to go to university. An aunt of mine said that this time 'I really had gone too far' and was too ambitious for my disability and educational abilities. There is a very firm belief by those in authority that a disabled person should, at all costs, have a 'secure' although boring and dull, job and once this has been secured then that is one's niche for life. I knew that I could never live such a fate and keep my sanity. I resolved to redress the imbalance of my early education. This proved a formidable task.

There are very few technical colleges that will accept a student without 'O' levels and certainly not if they are a poorly educated and disabled person who already has a good job with the Civil Service. I applied to college after college, went to interview after interview. Sometimes my lack of education was used as an excuse for those not wishing to take a disabled student. I was told that I could not climb the stairs involved, despite having just walked up them. Some blatantly stated that I was lucky to have such a good secretarial job in the past particularly being disabled — I should be grateful, should forget wanting to be anything else and would not get into university anyway. Eventually I went privately to a career guidance centre to see if I was overreaching myself. The analyst said I had potential to do 'other' things but that my disability precluded these and secretarial work in the Civil Service was the best place for me as it was secure. Rather than pacifying me and encouraging feelings of security, it only added fuel to the burning desire to 'better' myself but I did not know how or what form it would take. I felt I was moving down a long black tunnel with no light at the end and no one willing to reach out and help.

I have been blessed in my life with extraordinary good friends and these have always been my life-lines and without them I flounder. They encouraged me to reach and fulfil my own expectations despite my disability and poor education. Eventually a technical college took a chance and decided to enrol me for 'A' levels. I am sure the head of department felt sorry for me having applied to so many places and failed. My friends encouraged me to apply for university even if it meant going to one and banging, literally, on the door and demanding acceptance. I had been brought up to think that I had nothing to offer the world but to accept the role that society decreed, with pity thrown in for good measure. I could never bang on anyone's door and demand entrance but I resolved that I would have something to offer so that I would not be refused.

I gained my 'A' levels and the following year entered university as a mature student. It was worth every inch of the battle. I discovered myself intellectually. Everyone is worth something however small and nothing is so satisfying as self-fulfilment. Although society cares to give me the stigma of being a disabled person, my own self-fulfilment allows me to lay that aside as an unimportant matter. For many disabled people who have never been encouraged to succeed in anything and are forced to wear such a label, it can often take them over so that all one sees is a disability and not a person. Everyone in life needs encouragement and needs to gain confidence in themselves and for me, university was that watershed. Whether one feels oppressed by the stigma of disability, forced into a sexist role or whatever, the important thing is that one is never alone and others can and do feel the same. But above all, one must be oneself as much as possible.

RACHEL

Rachel, who is 38, has epilepsy. She trained as a nurse and midwife prior to becoming a ward sister of a busy surgical ward. Her interest in education grew when she was invited to take a post as a teacher of pupil nurses and from there she undertook a training at London University for the Sister Tutor's Diploma following on with a degree in psychology and philosophy. She is now a senior tutor in a London teaching hospital. Her interests include voluntary work for St John Ambulance Brigade and for this work she was admitted as a serving sister to the Order of St John in 1979. She is a member of the local parochial church council, a governor of a local school and an active member of the British Epilepsy Association. She lives in London with her husband.

Most professional nurses would agree that there are many rewards in their jobs other than security and promotion prospects. In my former work as a senior ward sister a fundamental psychological need within me was fulfilled. A desire to nurse had first entered my mind at two years of age and had remained with me throughout my career. At last after years of waiting I was doing the work that I had always wanted to do. I was happy and contented and working long and sometimes hard and difficult hours. The privilege one had of helping the sick to get well again or the permanently

disabled to come to terms with their disability or the dying
to die in peace and with dignity was the most wonderful
experience for me and one that I felt I could do for the
rest of my life. Deep down inside me I really believed that
this is what I was put on this earth to do and I studied constantly to improve my knowledge and skills.

My home life was just as full and as exciting as my work.
I had a house and a car, I did a lot of voluntary work for the
St John Ambulance Brigade; took leading comedy parts in
the local drama group and helped to run the Sunday school
for the church. My health had always been good, with only
five days' sick leave in my whole career.

On 7 December 1967 this life style came to an abrupt end
when quite out of the blue whilst on duty one afternoon I
had a grand mal epileptic seizure. Once the diagnosis of
temporal lobe epilepsy was confirmed, matron informed
me that I was medically unfit to nurse. The doctor had interviewed my parents, telling them that in his opinion I would
possibly have to take anticonvulsant drugs regularly for the
rest of my life. He advised my mother that I would be best
living with someone who was willing to take care of me
making sure that I took the drugs at the right time and that
I did not get into places which might prove dangerous should
I start a fit. Mother immediately said I was to go home and
live with them. At the same time both my parents were
extremely distressed at both the diagnosis and the prognosis.
It was very traumatic for me to see my dear parents so upset.

I gave hours of intensive thought about what line of action
I should take. The fits were frequent and irregular but I
became quite convinced that at all costs I must endeavour to
lead a normal independent life. I did not agree with the
doctor's idea of the management of the case. Being basically
an honest straight-forward sort of person I told the doctor
that I did not agree with him and consequently made an
enemy for life. My request for a second medical opinion was
agreed and arranged but once again concern was expressed
about my apparent lack of acceptance of the epilepsy; this

made me really quite angry because I failed to see how anyone could not accept it since the fits interfered with my
daily life very much. The second medical opinion confirmed
everything that had already been said with the exception that
the second doctor said he could see no reason why I should
not attempt to train as a teacher providing I understood that
there would be restrictions on certain types of teaching. I
asked if I could become one of his patients but he said he
was shortly leaving the area to take up a post in Manchester.
My fight was now on. I was going to train for a teacher
and nothing was going to stop me.

The fits continued and I kept being admitted to hospital.
Lying in the hospital ward I had time to think. I cried a
lot because I was now really beginning to miss my job. I
thought about some of my ex-patients who would be returning to the ward for more surgery. One evening three old
patients called to see me. This was more than I could stand
and they had to leave prematurely. I was at a very low ebb
because I felt so horribly alone. The staff didn't seem to
know how to talk to me. I tried to chat to the nurses but
sister would call them away, she was still very angry with me
because I had argued with the consultant and asked for a
new doctor to look after me. One morning quite spontaneously I refused Holy Communion. The chaplain looked
annoyed but said, 'That's all right.' I knew jolly well it wasn't
all right and began to feel guilty, but at the same time realised that I must take a grip of myself. I must have faith in
God if I was going to gain any strength in myself at all.

The anticonvulsant drugs made me very drowsy. If I sat
in a chair I would fall asleep for long hours and then awake
with a pool of wet and dry saliva down my front. Medical
advice said that I had to choose between the control of the
fits or a drowsy state. I decided to keep taking the high dose
but to walk whenever I could, to stop myself falling asleep.
It was very hard going but it worked. My first success at
rehabilitation was all my own work. I felt elated that at
long last I was achieving something. I was living in my house,

doing my housework and shopping and getting in with society again. Within a very short time, I learned that society found grand mal epilepsy upsetting, distasteful, frightening and that I was becoming a local nuisance. My behaviour during a fit made people think of insanity because I made strange noises and after fixing my eyes would then start to roll them. Oddly enough no one in hospital had ever told me how I behave whilst unconscious. It would have been such a help if they had, because I did not wish to frighten people and when I realised I was doing just that it was very sad. Upon awaking from a fit people might be comforting each other or telling me in an aggressive way that I had no right to go out on my own in such a bad way.

I hadn't realised that I was causing all this unrest locally. Some people were very sympathetic and kind, some could not understand my attitude. My attitude towards the fits was that they were very inconvenient because they were so unpredictable and left one feeling absolutely dreadful in the sense that one felt drowsy, nauseated, thirsty, cold and damp. Damp because during a fit I am copiously incontinent of urine and sometimes incontinent of faeces. Bystanders to such an event, quite rightly so, found this extremely unpleasant.

More important to me than my own attitude to epilepsy was the attitude of my friends and work colleagues. They were all very shocked about what had happened to me and basically could not see how I might manage a job or further training. I became very annoyed with this negative attitude because as a ward sister, whenever any of my patients had to cope with a disability or retrain for other employment, I not only encouraged them, but if they needed me to help or support, I considered it very much part of my role to do so. This sudden realisation that there were, in the National Health Service, professional people who could not see beyond the clinical condition to the psychological and sociological implications of the disorder, shocked me at first beyond words and then verbally I became very fluent on the matter. Thirteen years later I am still appalled at this aspect of patient care. I consider it the duty of all professional people dealing with disability of a long-term or chronic nature to meet the patients and their relatives and friends and to learn from them the needs of the patient. Professions must, before giving advice on 'aftercare' be taught by those who have a deep understanding and experience. Patient organisations serve a very useful purpose in this area. For me the British Epilepsy Association is doing this job with the utmost tact and efficiency.

In the early days most of my professional friends thought I was either highly ambitious or just plain mad when I talked of enjoying life again. I planned a trip to Scotland and stated that when I returned I would have decided upon a new life, going up, over or round any obstacle that got in my way. Talk got round that I was becoming aggressive when I discussed hospital care, self-centred when I talked of future employment and manic when I had learned to laugh at the various situations which I inevitably got into. I argued back, which in one sense was the worst thing to do, because before being ill I had been an extremely gentle and placid person. This all confirmed a change of personality. It was most frustrating because for me it was this new hostile environment that I now found myself in, which had brought about my reaction, not the epilepsy. Fortunately prior to 1967 I had never been in opposition to anyone.

It seemed to me that the doctors and nurses looking after me had a most appalling lack of insight into the problems of a patient with epilepsy and I told them so. I also told the matron, who told me I was just a trouble-maker. Her new deputy heard this conversation and came to my room later to tell me in a most gentle way, to keep my Christian faith and be patient, because I would not always be looked after by people who did not understand. I was amazed at what she was saying. In her quiet way she left me wondering if I had dreamed the last ten minutes. The deputy matron had also seen my mother and had likewise given my parents some positive comfort. When I see people now who are new to epilepsy I try to have the same approach to them as that deputy matron had to me and my relatives.

Sister, because I repeatedly kept coming back into hospital, suggested to my mother that I should stop trying to fight the inevitable. Mother became very distressed and it was obvious that the conflicting ideas of sister and myself were beginning to take their toll of her, so I went home with my parents. Doctor and sister explained to them that I should lead a quiet life, free from anxiety because worry and anxiety might precipitate the fits. This time I really lost my temper with them. I refused to do this. I was going to lead a normal life and take my responsibility in the world like any other fully fledged adult. It was true that I would take the drugs regularly as prescribed. I would not take alcohol or drive a car or put myself physically in any position which would prove dangerous to me should I fit. Apart from that I was going to be little old hard-working me, if only to prove them wrong! I cannot remember ever being so angry with anyone like this before. I told my consultant that I would use the media to try to give confidence to disabled people — to go out into the world and develop into people with the confidence to do their own individual thing in contributing to society, because I felt that the professionals would not help them in this way. My empathy for the sick had increased so much. I also told doctor this and he told me that I had got most things out of proportion again. I was livid.

Living with my parents was difficult because they saw too many fits. I had managed to keep the frequency of the fits away from them while living at my own place. My fits were bad. Sometimes I would fall all the way downstairs or bang my head on the nice oak furniture or fall in the street, so mother's neighbours started to talk, as my own neighbours had done. My parents did not sleep very well at night because sometimes I would fit in the night and they would hear me and come to me. Mother would come into my room every time she heard me turn over in bed, thinking that I was unwell. I sensed the strain on them both and returned to my house where they visited me frequently. My mother had developed an intermittent loss of memory which she still has.

On returning home I went through a patch of really long-lasting fits. This was new and worried me a great deal. Was it possible that I could be getting worse? It had never occurred to me that that could happen. Over a period of six days I had sixteen fits as far as I could count, then I passed into *status epilepticus* (passing from one fit into another without gaining consciousness). I owe my life to the very same professional people whom I had fought with so much. Their skill at managing the acute situation was, and still is, of the highest order.

I gained consciousness with their superb care and drug therapy. Sister came on duty and said, 'Hello, I see you have been misbehaving again.' I felt terrible but because they had saved my life, I could not bring myself to tell her that nurses did not speak to sick people as though they were public trouble-makers. Sister turned to a pupil nurse and said, 'Stay with her, she's really bad this time and we don't know if she will go into *status* again.' This time I couldn't contain myself, so I replied, 'We sick patients do not need to be told how bad we are, Sister. Such news delays our progress.' 'You be quiet and do as you are told', she said. The pupil nurse came in and she started to cry. She was the very same girl I had taught surgical nursing. Despite a drip in my arm and ECG leads on my chest, I managed to put my arm around her and give her a paper tissue to dry her eyes. 'Oh Sister', she said, 'Why did this have to happen to you?' At the name 'Sister', I started to cry. 'What is going to happen to you?' she said. 'You always will be my favourite Sister, I wish I could help you.' During this time the film *Sound of Music* was very popular, so I tried to comfort her by saying, 'Well, nurse, you know what it says in the *Sound of Music*, "When the Lord closes a door He opens a window". I am just looking for my open window, it's going to turn up some day and in the meantime, we must just wait.' A staff nurse was passing by, she rushed in almost shouting at the pupil nurse, 'What's this she is saying about jumping out of a window?' Nurse wept loudly and was removed by two nurses. Sister came. Staff nurse reported that she had overheard me telling the nurse that I was going to jump out of the window. Sister said, 'We must inform doctor and matron.' The deputy matron came instead. The pupil nurse had told her the whole story and she said I was not to worry, it was just a misunderstanding. The ward lights were out, it was nearly midnight. She told me that the junior consultant whom I had worked for and herself were trying to get me into teaching. She said I was to trust them and to carefully consider going to London to train because she had contacts at the National Hospital for Nervous Diseases and she was certain that once I was living in London that hospital would be very willing to look after me. It all seemed very strange to me. I wouldn't really mind going to London, I would be able to attend the Old Vic regularly which would be super.

Next morning a new doctor called to see me and enquire about what I had said the night before about jumping out of the window. I told him what had happened and suggested that he contacted the pupil nurse. 'She's gone off sick,' he said. 'Are you a psychiatrist?' I asked, 'Because if so, I wish to see what has been written in my notes.' He showed me. A note had been added regarding a possible thought of suicide. He asked me if I was depressed, adding that if he had my little lot he would be. 'That just goes to show that you are more unstable than I. No, I have no intention of leaving this world until I have done something about the care that patients get to enable them to go out into the world with their disabilities and live active useful lives.' He left me without telling whether or not he was a psychiatrist — I looked him up in the medical directory later and found out that he was! Next day my own doctor called to see me and spoke to sister. 'Did Doctor ——— prescribe

her any antidepressant drugs?' Sister said he didn't. 'I want
her to have some when she goes home.' Six months later he
told me how much better I looked and he felt it was largely
due to the combination of antidepressants and anticonvul-
sants. I told him I disagreed because I had never cashed the
antidepressant prescription and had no intention of ever
taking any such drugs. I never went back to see him — I
dare not go because he was so angry that day. I think I am
bad for his health. From then on things got better and
better for me. The fits occurred only two or three times per
week, the drowsy state got better and every time I thought I
was going to fall asleep I walked a mile or so and got over it.
I was accepted by the first college that I applied to. The
professor told me that everyone would be most helpful
should the fits occur in college but for my part I had to
maintain a high academic standard as no concessions could
be given to me if my standard of work became poor. To be
accepted was a terrific ego boost. In September 1969 I
started. The newness of London suited me fine, very few
people knew my medical history, I started to use my other
christian name because I just wanted to forget the past. It
all worked so well, I got interested in many things, joined
various student clubs, started drama again, got elected to the
local church PCC and made London my home — as it turned
out for ever, because I later married a London man and we
are very happy living and working within London. The
National Hospital for Nervous Diseases look after me and
their kindness and understanding is of the highest order. All
that I am now, I owe to them, to my professor and my
college tutor, I obviously could not fight on my own, I
needed people who understood epilepsy and understood me.

As the teacher training came to an end I had to start looking for work, someone tipped me off that a school in London
had a principal whose mother was epileptic. One person on
the interview panel was not at all happy about employing
me, but the principal won the argument; three years later I
got into the London teaching hospitals.

I know now that to be stretched in one's job is right. Drugs have to be taken with absolute regularity in order to maintain a uniform blood level of drug, no alcohol can be taken. The latter is really quite tough because at parties one remains stone cold sober and consequently observes all sorts of behaviour and eventually gets bored with it all! Sometimes people try to encourage one to indulge, once or twice I have discovered my fruit juice laced with alcohol. That annoys me very much. I take my pills regularly in the loo because it saves answering questions or being said to be very neurotic. Actually they taste dreadful so I would prefer to take them with a nice cup of tea.

For years now I have had an aura before a grand mal fit. The aura is tingling in my left arm, and I lose consciousness about two minutes later. This gives me plenty of time to get myself into a safe place and hopefully a place on my own. I can then lie down on the floor, pull my skirts up to prevent them becoming wet with urine and then wait. Mostly I can be back in circulation within 30 minutes. It is better however, if I can lie down for a little longer because I feel pretty rotten. In the daily routine it is not always possible to rest. My fits now are very well controlled and have occurred during the night mostly. I am also prone to petit mal fits. These fits are very short absences, i.e. of a few seconds. One does not even fall to the ground and no bodily harm is done. Most observers would not even be aware of anything happening. However, from a practical point of view it can be a great inconvenience because during an absence one is not aware of what is going on. For example, listening to a lecture, if a petit mal occurs, the message will be interrupted, thus altering the meaning. I have now learned to overcome this by, at lectures or meetings, taking meticulous notes and then comparing them with other facts on the event. Petit mals occur much more frequently than the grand mal. Therefore, it would be quite wrong for me to attempt to drive. If I have a petit mal when walking downstairs, I usually end up by falling down the rest of the stairs. Fortunately, people

do not think of the basic problem being epilepsy. If I have
a bad week, people may comment about my clumsiness but
that is certainly the lesser of the two evils.

JUNE

June, who is 38 years old, is an only child and was born and
lived for the first five years of her life in India. She has severe
cerebral palsy, incurred through injuries at birth, and can
live in the community only with the continual help of atten-
dants. She has a BA Honours in psychology and a postgraduate diploma in youth and community work. Her work
experience has included being a warden of a hostel for home-
less boys, running a night shelter for boys, a club for 'Hell's
Angels' and a spell in a drug addiction centre. June now lives
in Manchester. She is a part-time tutor with the Open University and a full-time mother.

'How could you do it?' was a question which had many
nuances and was put to me by many people, during and
after my pregnancy. The GP wondered how I could have
had intercourse in my 'predicament' (as a good friend invariably describes my situation). The gynaecologist wondered
how it was socially possible for me to bring up a child, and
social services merely stood on the side-lines, not offering
any practical help but making me feel they were wondering
how I would maintain myself and my child in the community, waiting for the first opportunity to take my child
away from me. I went so far as to ban the social worker
from the house after my baby was born because they had
been so unhelpful to me during my pregnancy and I did not
wish to support their professional voyeurism. You see, not
only was it immoral to be an unmarried mother but it was
doubly immoral to be an unmarried mother AND a severely

disabled person daring to produce a child — a normal, healthy, beautiful child.

However, they were not the only people asking questions — my head never stopped buzzing with them. The first question was the physical safety of the child and myself if the pregnancy was to be continued. I arranged to see my orthopaedic surgeon in Sheffield. His genuine pleasure and reassurance when he heard of my pregnancy gave me great comfort at a time when the only word I was hearing was abortion. This man, Mr Sherrard, has my greatest admiration for his sensitivity, patience and compassion. Once I was assured of the safety of the baby and myself, my friend's words rang in my ears and my resolution to have a very wanted but unplanned baby was made stronger.

The gist of the discussion we had had a few years previously had been that one should not wait for 'the right moment' to have a child for this 'right moment' rarely came. My friend, who was not disabled, had her child two years before I became pregnant. She, like myself, was not married. While thinking of her words I remembered the numerous times I had been told I could not do something and had proved everyone wrong — for example going to university and living in the community with the assistance of an au pair and fellow students. However, I did not minimise the difficulties that would face me.

Other questions passing rapidly and constantly through my mind were from where I would obtain my helpers, how I would pay them and how I would accommodate them adequately. I realised that I would have to employ two helpers — one to look after me and one to look after my baby — and that the two-bedroomed private flat I rented at the time would not be adequate for four adults and a baby. My boyfriend was living with me at the time. Thank God, I was surrounded by staunch long-standing friends and relatively new ones who were morally and practically supportive. They spent many hours in libraries looking up charities I could apply to for extra money and many more long hours helping me to write letters to them, my MP and social security. I also put my name down immediately for a four-bedroomed council house, as I felt that the two helpers deserved their privacy as their hours of work would be long and the emotional and psychological stress would be great. In fact, I received a three-bedroomed council house when my son was eighteen months old. Eventually, when I felt it was psychologically bad for my son not to have his own 'personal space', my helpers had to share a room thus reducing their privacy and their 'personal space'. This produced its own traumas and eventually led to an irrevocable crisis which has only recently been satisfactorily resolved.

My applications to numerous charities proved fruitless and initially I had to rely on the extra — but inadequate — money my MP obtained for me from social security. Later with the aid of a sympathetic and relentless welfare rights officer, to whom I am much indebted, I embarked on a long and complicated battle with socal security which has only just ended in a final tolerably satisfactory payment for myself and helpers.

The next hurdle was finding the helpers! Fortunately for my baby and myself a friend in the block of flats where I was living was an English teacher and had taught and made friends with an au pair the previous year who wished to return to England during her summer holidays. She was German, clean, efficient and capable. She gave my baby the best start in life for which I could ever have hoped. After Ursula, who became a good friend and the baby's godmother, had left, my unending search for au pairs began. Only two agencies, out of the many I contacted throughout the country, were sympathetic to my specialist needs. Au pairs are only allowed to work five hours a day and I and my baby needed constant attention. Ursula also worked hard in Germany, finding me an agency, who supplied me with suitable girls at spasmodic intervals. There followed an ever-increasing number of girls — mainly French and German, with an equal number of crises, before the arrival of one or the departure of another. Some were excellently efficient, others tried hard, while a few were totally incompetent. Their period of employment ranged from nine months to one week, while recently two eighteen-year-olds beat the record by staying the course for the great duration of three hours! They were, in fact, from the Italian Riviera so that Moss Side, an Inner City area with a high immigrant and generally poor population, must have been quite a shock for them! Finally, the agency from whence came these girls retracted their invaluable service in January 1980 and I was left with no other sources to which to turn. Fortunately, a long-suffering friend came to my rescue and offered to help out for a short while. Seven months later, not only is she still here but she is looking after myself and my small son, virtually single-handed, while a long and arduous battle has ensued between myself and social services.

When my au pair source 'dried up' I turned to a voluntary organisation, Community Service Volunteers, who run a 'one-to-one' project with disabled people, helping them to live in the community. However social services are reluctant to make a small monetary commitment. This is very frustrating as the contribution they are being asked to make is a mere 'drop in the ocean' compared with the commitment they would have to make if they took my son and myself into care!

My pregnancy was normal and healthily boring. I had no strange cravings, high blood pressure or any of the other symptoms associated with pregnancy, which I was expected to have. The only discomfort I suffered was 'night sickness' for the whole nine months and not being able to drink alcohol. This latter affliction caused great frustration to myself and great merriment to my friends. There is nothing more frustrating or irritating than seeing drunken friends through sober eyes at parties, wishing you could be equally drunk and equally stupid. I was, at the time, at college doing my postgraduate diploma in youth and community work.

Being pregnant did not stop me from doing any of the things I was used to doing — from hitching down to London during my fourth month, to going out to parties and generally socialising, or working on placements. I felt that being pregnant was not a reason for opting out and many arguments ensued with my tutor, who felt that I should not exert myself doing placements because it was bad for my health and unfair on the baby. On the contrary, my arguments were that as I had never felt healthier or more fit it was ludicrous to sit around languishing and brooding when there were so many interesting things to do and so little time in which to do them. Besides this, not many mothers or 'mothers-to-be' could afford the luxury of lying around being pregnant. I was even more aware of this than usual because I had just finished working with single-parent families on a council estate. My placement had been to 'set up' a club for them, with the help of another student on our course.

The real stress during my pregnancy was of an emotional and psychological nature. Although both my boyfriend and myself did not believe in abortion and I had made a positive decision to give birth to and keep my baby, we were both very very 'scared' about the future and how we would overcome the problems mentioned above. His natural reaction was not to talk about it or plan for it in any way — in fact to pretend it wasn't happening. This was partly my reaction as well because when I thought of the future I became panic-stricken and overwhelmed at the enormity of what I was 'taking on'. However, at the same time, I felt resentful at not being able to enjoy my pregnancy and plan together with him the coming of our baby. I confided this to a nurse, during my last few weeks in hospital. She assured me that this was very normal and that throughout her pregnancy all her husband wanted was a dog! I had to have a caesarian section and although my baby was a healthy 5lb 13½oz boy, it was hospital policy to keep caesarian section babies in an incubator for twenty-four hours. Thus the only person to see him in the first twenty-four hours was 'his dad'. After gazing at his son for twenty minutes he tore himself away to announce that he was the most beautiful baby he had ever seen.

The hospital staff were incredibly sympathetic and spared no efforts to help all three of us. The gynaecologist, after he had lost his two-hour-long abortion battle, refused to co-operate on any issues with me. I was fortunate because two of my friends were pregnant at the same time as me and were able to advise me. When I asked my gynaecologist for a prescription to prevent my sickness, his answer was, 'That's what being pregnant is all about, and you wanted to be pregnant!' He was also horrified because I expressed a wish to breast-feed my baby and categorically refused to allow it. However the nursing staff said it was none of his business and promised to do everything in their power to assist me. I think all the staff were pleased to be witnessing such an out-of-the-ordinary type of confinement and, thus, were only too eager to help me in any way. I was also fortunate in that there were not too many confinements and births at this time so that the staff were not rushed off their feet. Also, I was in hospital for six weeks before my baby was born, owing to premature contractions, so that the staff were familiar with the situation.

When they brought my baby to me I just could not believe that this tiny perfect being with a mass of dark hair, tiny clenched fists and a little red face was really mine. I had helped to give him life. I had nurtured him for nine months inside me and now here he was, a reality, the most precious gift I had ever been given. Suddenly I knew that all I had gone through to make him possible and all that I would go through in the future to ensure a happy, healthy, loving and fulfilling life for him was worth every effort. I had no problems in breast-feeding, apart from finding the best position to hold him. He was a very adaptable baby and I successfuly fed him myself for three months. For me, this was one of the most wonderful experiences of my life and created that bond between us that might otherwise not have been formed, because of the sheer practicalities of the situation. I could not do one physical thing for my son unaided. For a long time I could not really believe that I was his mother and that he was really my offspring. I think most mothers feel this during the first post-natal months but the constant attention required by a new-born baby soon makes this a reality, because, I am sure, only a mother could do this. Now my child is nearly four years old and the wonder of knowing he is mine is no less. Now the physical attention he needs from others is less, and the emotional and psychological support he needs from me is greater. Thus the bond between us becomes stronger daily.

The future is uncertain for everyone but for me it is a hundred per cent more uncertain and from long and bitter experience I have learned not to look too far into it. However, there are a few things of which I am certain. No one will ever take Frank away from me. He will grow up in a happy and loving environment and will be as secure and as well adjusted as any other child with two 'able-bodied' parents. He will, however, have the advantage over other children because his sensitivity and tolerance will have been heightened by his environment and hopefully, he will learn to live life to the full and be sensitive to the plight of others. My last wish for the future is that although Frank is the most precious thing in my life, when he is old enough to lead his own life he will feel free to do so and not be pressurised by feelings of guilt or misguided 'duty' to stay at home and look after me. I have led a full and relatively happy life and this is the legacy I would like to give to my son.

DIANA — I

Diana, who is 39, had a very severe attack of polio when she was 13 years old. She was paralysed from head to foot

and spent four weeks in an iron lung. Her next three years
were spent in hospital at Oxford, where fortunately there
was a hospital school. From there she went on to a college
for disabled people to do a secretarial course and eventually
into her first job. Over the years she has gained a great deal
of independence and now drives an ordinary adapted car.
However, she has only one working arm, very weak legs
and shaky balance. She can only walk sort distances on
crutches and is much safer using the back of her wheelchair when she can sit or walk as she pleases. She now lives
and works in London and has recently married.

For the disabled woman who is career minded or just wants
to work, the difficulties placed in her way are not only the
physical ones of coping with the disability linked to the
access problems, but more often the subtle psychological
ones that can have a far greater effect on confidence and her
own awareness and understanding of her disability. My first
job lasted for twelve years, by which time I was aching to
move on, and had achieved a degree of independence that
would allow this. The low expectations of the Disabled
Resettlement Officer (DRO) I sought help from in this attempted move made me realise she had no idea of what I could
do and without actually saying so implied I should stay put
as I had a good job. My second job led on to a great deal
of confidence building by my boss which finally allowed
me to apply for a job which would mean commuting in and
out of London each day — something my family frowned
on, but allowed me to really test out my capabilities, leading
eventually to living in London.
   My work has always been in the health service in the rehabilitation side, for the first years in a spinal unit, where I
found myself identifying problems that newly disabled
people and their families needed help with in helping themselves, and then into a mental handicap hospital where I saw
similar problems. As this was a small hospital I had a lot of
contact with the families of mentally handicapped people

and learned a lot about their difficulties. From here I went on to develop in London the newly formed Spinal Injuries Association and had the opportunity to try out some of the ideas that had been gathering in the back of my mind whilst working in the spinal unit. I now work as part of a team looking at the needs of mentally handicapped, mentally ill, elderly or physically disabled, most of my work being concerned with physically disabled. Whilst the onset of disability seriously disturbed my own school career, the experience gained through various jobs and my own personal experience of disability help me in my present post. A lot of this work is concerned with attitudes to disability not only of professionals to disabled, but of disabled group to disabled group. My recent work has included a small project looking at employment for handicapped school leavers, and in talking to both these young people and the professionals helping them it has thrown up some interesting things about attitudes to the employment of handicapped people and the experiences of both professionals and employers.

My own first promotion came only because they were unable to find and keep a senior secretary prepared to take the rough and tumble of a busy medical office. After three girls had come and gone, and I had six months of combining my own work load with that of the consultant needing the new secretary, I ventured to ask if I could have the job. It had until that time never dawned on me that they had not noticed the extra work and administrative tasks I had absorbed and carried out without asking an undue number of questions, or things going wrong. I remember being a bit hurt about this, although it was something I was used to, as when being employed on a trial basis I had had it impressed upon me that I would have to work well with the others, this working well often meant I got the most of the 'nasty' jobs — not being able to run meant that I was left sitting when such a 'job' was seen coming towards the office. However I made my request, getting a surprised look and the comment, 'Oh, do you think you could manage?'

followed by, 'But it must go to the Hospital Management Committee for their decision.' I remember being upset by this, because I knew that no such decision was made on the other girls who had been employed for such short periods. I was also hurt that of the four girls in the office I was one of two who had secretarial qualifications and I felt strongly that this should mean more in my favour than it obviously did. I remember also thinking over the fact that the comments had been made that I would not be able to run certain errands, i.e. get x-rays, make office tea. These were all little things that appeared to be raised because of my chair, the fact that I got through more desk work on occasions than others seemed to get forgotten. The other thing that did disturb me and made me wonder if I was difficult to get on with was that I accidentally heard one of the consultants checking out how another felt about me having the post. This, I felt, said little for the doctors working in this rehabilitation unit dealing with disabled people, from where medical papers often appeared criticising other employers outside the health service. One thing I had always insisted on at work was that I was no different from the other girls. I took my fair share but it seemed to me that my simple request for the upgrading on the grounds that I was doing the work anyway had led to a full investigation within the office as to how I got on with people.

In the event I got the upgrading, and suddenly became aware of my own abilities and the fact that I could achieve much more, despite the fact that the other girls felt I should not have had the job and its responsibilities. It was OK while I was filling in, but once I was given the post — 'well, she's disabled isn't she!'

Some four years ago the hunt for jobs led to a very distressing interview which made me stop job-hunting and ask if I could rearrange my London job and hours to fit in with personal and family commitments. It also served to remind me that in some quarters 'things ain't changed'. I had gone for interview for an administrative assistant, again in the

health service. By the time I got to the interview board I
was feeling a bit tense because I had had to spend half
an hour trying to find the office in the hospital, not even
the receptionist at the front door knowing the interviews
were taking place. Additionally I had had to get help to get
down a flight of steps. I should have been warned by this
that although they had the information 'wheelchair user'
in front of them on the application form, no concessions
were to be made.

I am not certain if all disabled people feel it, but one is
often aware if the person talking to you is at ease or obviously discomforted by your disability. I always expect
to be dealt with in the same way as other candidates at interview, but it was very obvious these three gentlemen were not
at ease with me. The board consisted of a young personnel
officer, the area personnel officer and the doctor in whose
department the job was based. Most of the talking was done
by the younger personnel officer. He could see nothing but
my chair, worse still he could not even say the word wheelchair, pointing at my chair and saying, 'How will you manage
in that thing?' We progressed through the mechanics of how
I would arrange my office furniture to how much help the
DRO would give to make the front door of the office acces-
sible. My information on the help that employers can be
given on this subject seemed to be totally opposite to that
the personnel officer had, and after gently correcting his
information once (I had only recently given up a job that
included running an information service which included this
subject, information this gentleman had in front of him) and
getting an icy stare from the rest of the interview board, I
found myself closing up. I sat through his comments on the
fact that I should have been registered as a disabled person,
'It makes my job easier'. On questions about the actual job
I received a sharp 'What do you know?' on an area where
I had admitted my experience to be limited, and this was
followed by, 'We have young male candidates anxious to
gain experience.' I remember wondering at this point whether

he had difficulty in keeping female staff in the building, or whether the fact that I was wearing trousers labelled me women's lib. The only questions the doctor asked were 'Did I like music?' 'How did I drive a car?' and 'Why did I use the back of the chair to walk on because they used walking frames in the rehabilitation department?'

By this time I was, I knew, coming over in a very bad way, answering yes and no and making no attempt to expand on questions. I was furiously angry at the whole tone of the interview and the range of questions that had been put to me, which seemed to have little to do with the job they were trying to fill. I actually felt like a freak. How many able-bodied candidates are asked to explain how they would arrange their office furniture? I was also being talked down to and wondering how I could overcome this. No doubt had I come back at them it would have just enforced their view of disabled people as having chips on their shoulder. I was particularly angry at the personnel officer's lack of know-ledge about the help available to him via the DRO's office; this seemed to imply that the hospital was well below its quota for employing disabled people, a situation which he gave the impression he was anxious to maintain. It took some days to rid myself of the silly ideas that the inter-view had planted in my mind, did I really do a good job, was I really able to organise myself, did I get on with people and so on and so on. I actually had to talk these points through with another wheelchair user, who was able to understand the prejudice I had sensed and helped me to put it into proportion. His parting shot was that perhaps I had paved the way with that personnel officer for the next dis-abled candidate he interviews. I wonder?

During my working life I have had a number of job inter-views, but none so negative as this one and it was no real surprise when a letter arrived stating that none of those interviewed had been offered the post — it had been given to someone already in the department. A recent letter from someone who knew me during the school-leaving period at

Oxford and having heard of my marriage and what had happened to me in the past twenty years, wrote saying that they had never realised I could achieve so much. This statement linked into the comments made by one disabled girl I had interviewed on school leaving, confirmed my feelings that expectations for girls in wheelchairs leaving school (unless they are intellectually high flyers) are set very low.

KAREN

Karen was born in Salisbury, Wiltshire, in the 1940s, the eldest of four daughters. She was a perfectly healthy baby until the age of 2, when she developed a tumour on the spine and she is now a paraplegic. Her formal education did not start until she was 9 years old. Then she went through the usual process of special education, except it was perhaps more radical than most, in that she was encouraged to excel academically and became part of the community of the children's home in which the school was based. Four years in a residential centre/workshop for the physically handicapped followed until she 'escaped' to do a secretarial course.

In 1969 she came to London and lived on her own for the first time, working in the education and training department of the National Association of Youth Clubs. She was accepted to do a community and youth work course at Westhill College of Education in Birmingham in 1972 and looks back upon this as the most stimulating period of her life to date. On leaving Westhill she spent four years working for National PHAB (physically handicapped/able bodied), an organisation concerned with the social integration of the two groups. From there she ran a full-time youth centre for an outer London borough, but at the time of writing had dropped out to do her own thing. Karen has made a 3,000 mile trip

across the United States in a Greyhound bus. Her addiction
is making and flying kites and this has included going up
sixty feet on a man-lifting kite. Her unfulfilled ambition is
to go hot-air ballooning.

As a child I was never really aware of the fact that I was
different from a large percentage of the population, certainly not until I was a teenager. If, on occasion, I was
treated as someone special because it was thought that I
would not make old bones, my ego was such that I assumed
it was because people thought I was a nice person. I often
think that it is a pity that kids with handicaps are allowed
to get away with anti-social behaviour by virtue of their
disability. With the onset of adolescence and all the things
that go to make the early teens an unhappy period — acne,
a flat chest and the 'curse' — came also an awakening sexual
awareness, and the idea that perhaps I was not quite the same
as other girls. My unawareness of my disability until that
time can be attributed to the fact that all the pupils in my
school were handicapped, and the able-bodied children in
the home where the school was situated were so used to
seeing us around that it didn't seem to make any difference
to them.

However, as an adolescent I realised that boys do not react
in the same way to a girl in a wheelchair as they do to other
girls. It was when I left school at seventeen that this awareness really hit me. However, it was tempered by the fact that
I was in a residential centre for the handicapped and was
beginning to date boys who were also physically impaired,
although occasionally I did also date able-bodied boys from
the town. My mother did not help me during this period,
telling me to think of higher things, to look for spiritual
relationships, because any man who appeared to be attracted
to me must be perverted. I am sure that as a mother she
wanted to protect me.

In those far-off days of unenlightenment, it was considered
impossible for paraplegics to enjoy a sex life, that we should

not even think about it, and if we did, then we were not normal. Finally, at the age of twenty-one I experienced real love for the first time and suffered a year of agony and ecstasy. I wanted desperately to 'make it' with the boy in question, but I never did, for two reasons. Firstly, fear of rejection was now beginning to take hold, and secondly, if you lived in a residential centre you were unlikely to have a room of your own. So the fear of rejection together with the possibility of being caught in the act were very powerful preventatives and eventually we both went our separate ways. Another real problem for a person who is physically impaired by paraplegia, apart from certain physical deformities, is that you are likely to be incontinent and the thought of having an accident whilst making love can be very inhibiting and takes away any spontaneity. For me this obstacle was removed at the age of twenty-two, after an extensive medical review revealed that I could be bowel and bladder trained. How this had not been discovered before I don't know, but the psychological barriers were lifted and my independence improved.

A variety of romances followed, none terribly serious and some more of a platonic nature. During this time I also left the residential centre, came to London and became involved in youth work. I finally lost my virginity at twenty-eight just before going to college. Even so, it took the guy in question six months of sensitive and gentle persuasion and then the occasion was for me a joyful and enjoyable one, coupled with a sense of relief. Most important of all, I was not rejected. I believe that because we took so long we knew each other well and my physical appearance really ceased to be of prime importance. After four years of living together we broke up finally not because of sexual incompatability but because of my boredom with him. I simply fell out of love. It was a feeling of guilt, and perhaps failure which made me stay with him so long. Acquaintances who did not know me well assumed, as is often the case, that he had left me and not the other way round, because I had a handicap and he had not. I did learn from the relationship that I did not have to feel grateful because a man loved me, and that a woman can, if she wants, call the tune in a relationship. I am still an incurable romantic and idealist, but increasing years have made me realise that if I did settle for one man, he would need to be the sort of person who would allow me to continue in the freedom I have gained in the last few years. Disabled women have the same spectrum of emotions able-bodied women have, but they, and other people, don't always realise it. You have to believe in yourself before others will believe in you.

ELSA

Elsa was born in Northern Rhodesia (now Zambia) in 1939 and attended a co-ed government school there before going on to Rhodes University in South Africa to read Latin and English. She broke her back in 1957 (complete fracture at T11/12, which means she is paralysed from below the waist) and had rehabilitation at Stoke Mandeville, England. The following year she married. After the divorce she lived with her parents on a smallholding in Rhodesia. She has lived in East London for the past eleven years since joining her mate here (she was an old school friend).

Her chief interest is writing fiction, short stories, novels, plays in which fantasy and reality are set side by side, and she is a member of Gay Authors Workshop which tries to raise the standard and range of gay writings. She is a founder member of Gemma, which is a group of disabled and able-bodied lesbians, formed in 1976, to provide a linking and information service for isolated disabled lesbians as well as attempting to increase awareness about disabled gays among the gay community and society generally. Elsa also works locally with the Campaign for Homosexual Equality and with

the East London Gay Liberation Front.

A lot of this will seem contradictory because I feel differently about my disability at different times, in the same day I have several different reactions to it. I don't think I've accepted completely my body's state and difficulties; I get tired of the routine of looking after it even though I know that the smallest neglect might result in trouble such as a pressure sore; now and then I seem unable to resist the temptation to treat it as 'normal', to skip a routine inspection of skin, to expect more than is possible, e.g. sitting up too long even when I know the skin on my bottom is in poor condition.

When I was first disabled I wouldn't look at my body, especially the legs. I left off my glasses so that I couldn't see it when the nurses washed and turned me. Looking back I am surprised that rejection of my body began so soon after my injury, before the muscles atrophied. After twenty-three years of disability I don't feel wholly resigned to my body the way it is, thin unshapely legs, navvy-like shoulders and torso (just as if tomorrow it might somehow regain a more conventionally acceptable shape). Sometimes I hanker for clothes I could have worn before but which would be uncomfortable and impractical for me now. I look at catalogues and half-plan to buy, knowing perfectly well I will stick to my blouses and slacks which suit me both aesthetically and practically. I have worn dresses and skirts a few times but I don't feel at ease in them, my waist isn't narrow now and they hamper my movement. With trousers I can dress/undress quickly, get in and out of cars, on/off toilet, etc. more freely. When I do wear dresses/skirts it is only for a short time, like party-going, and it is like dressing up for a joke. For everyday life I need loose clothing that I can forget, easy to get on and off, and which hides my shape as much as possible. In this camouflage I suspect I imagine that my body underneath is the same as it was.

My image of myself is not clear because for so many years

I avoided thinking about this. In one way I feel my wheel-chair is part of me and I resent people leaning on it, fiddling with it. I accept it and I ignore it. I feel irritated when atten-tion is drawn to it — 'What a nice wheelchair!' I suppose I should respond as sensibly as if a car or bicycle were being praised. It was quite a shock to me recently to discover my blind spot about myself; I needed a picture of a woman in a wheelchair from which I might make an illustration, and I was hunting through magazines for some time before it occurred to me I need only look in my own photo album — there I am, in a wheelchair. Why after so long don't I see myself as a wheelchair-user? It looks as if even to me 'wheel-chair people' are other people and not me.

Early in my disability I had a rejecting attitude towards other disabled and have only just got rid of this (though not entirely, it would seem). I didn't then want to mix with dis-abled people, didn't want to be associated with them, I wanted to pass for non-disabled, as it were. I wanted des-perately to be accepted as 'normal'. Having no information about gay people, I didn't even know able-bodied lesbians could have a happy purposeful life, and after my injury I rejected my sexual orientation and took on the role of being heterosexual. I saw marriage and children as the best way to prove to my family and anyone else that I was a 'real' person. I can remember a sort of terror at being allotted forever to the 'single' category, and at being pitied for being single. I wanted to be part of the herd, with a partner like other women. At school and college I had been a loner with few friends. Disability suddenly made this unbearable. I couldn't bear that my disability would seem the reason for my singleness. At that time it brought out the worst in me, senselessly and needlessly I was fighting a peculiar hurtful and selfish campaign for survival, I seemed to think that if I could pass as a housewife and mother everything would be all right. Fortunately I wasted only a few years in this dangerous way.

Disability forced me to talk more (hitherto I was not

extrovert), I felt and still do feel that I have to keep proving I'm not mentally disabled as well. I still open conversations deliberately to dispel any suspicion I might be mentally retarded. I don't entirely approve of the chatty personality I seem to have developed for this. Since having a friend with Down's syndrome, however, I feel less the urge to dissociate myself from mentally disabled people. So what if I am taken for one of them, they also have the right to go about the world. Now that I meet more disabled people, particularly other disabled lesbians, I enjoy some feeling of solidarity with them though I still feel I am not a 'proper disabled person'. I compare myself unfavourably with the stereotype, a disabled person who struggles against the odds to complete her education, get a job, play sport, drive a car, travel, etc., and do a good PR job with 'the public', explaining competently about disability. I feel myself inferior to this image and at the same time know it is ridiculous, we have the right to be the sort of people we are, disabled or not. It annoys me when able-bodied people hold forth about how we should be as independent as possible — of course we should be but I'd like to hear some talk about the able-bodied being a bit more independent too — how many of them even cut their own hair, for goodness sake, and how many of them with full use of all their senses can occupy themselves for twelve hours without resorting to laid-on entertainment. No wonder we're asked, 'What do you do with yourself all day? I suppose you *read* a lot,' or a patronising, doubtful, 'Well, you seem to keep busy.' This even if the disabled person has full use of hands, eyes and brain. Their inadequacies are projected onto us.

Not being expected to do a full-time paid job benefited me in one way; it meant I had time to devote to my fiction writing, art and handcrafts. Mainly for my family's sake I wish I had more material success in these fields, though I think that as soon as I was disabled their expectations of me ceased. I haven't told my family I work with the Gemma group — and I think they would regard this sort of work with a disabled group as very much second best — pretend work. I partly subscribe to this, observing how much other people dislike working and feel I have 'got away with it'. Work should be unpleasant or boring, and what I do is neither. I half believe even a tedious job would be 'better' because that would bring in money and be socially acceptable — illogically perhaps I would be proud of doing such a job, uncreative and stultifying though it might be.

When I came to live with my lesbian mate I felt a bit absurd about being gay *and* disabled. With her I was at ease of course, but I felt self-conscious about meeting other lesbians, I thought they'd see me as non-sexual, they'd think 'how can she be gay like us'. When I was passing for heterosexual it didn't occur to me to think I'd be regarded as non-sexual — I think this is because I saw heterosexual women as sexually passive anyway, whereas I see lesbians as sexual equals.

Since writing to and meeting other Gemma members I have become confident about my identity as a disabled gay. But I think it is well that this relationship (of eleven years' standing now) is the only one I want. I don't think I could ever embark upon another one. She and I had known each other for years before we lived together so I was close to her anyway. Even so, it was a gradual process introducing her to my physical problems. In the first years I wasn't happy about her helping me, for instance, when toilets were inaccessible and I had to use a bowl. Now I'm not embarrassed about it but I still wonder, is this really nice for her, could year upon year of this affect our relationship? These are only half-serious doubts. I have phases of asking her for reassurance (knowing I will get it), childish direct questions: 'Am I grotesque?' She is half-exasperated, half-amused. I trust her completely, I know she won't laugh at my body as one nurse did once. If we did separate I couldn't put the same trust in someone else, I could never start all over again, I'd be too afraid of rejection/disgust, it would take too long for me to get as close to someone else again.

I notice I have an ambivalent attitude towards more

information about disability being generally available. On one hand I want everyone to understand more, yet illogically I find I don't want them to have the physical details of what *I* have to do each day, my bladder management, my manual evacuation. I suppose I shall grow out of this feeling of having lost privacy.

Because I have many varied interests, perhaps because I associate my disability with the growing and developing part of my young adulthood, I don't long to be able-bodied again, except on a few occasions, when with uncongenial company and I wish I could escape quickly, or when I want some shopping in a hurry. I feel that when I was able-bodied I was a self-centred, inactive sort of person and that I would have continued in that way. It's as if being able-bodied were my larval or pupal stage and being disabled is the real me now. Though disability has probably shortened my life it has given me a good deal by changing its direction, forcing me to communicate and sensitising me to other people's lives. It is one of the reasons I joined the animal liberation movement; seeing pictures of monkeys in restraint chairs, sows chained to the floor, makes me relive my first claustrophobic horrors when I had to lie as staff had positioned me.

In two respects at least I had to view my disablement positively. My adolescence was plagued with severe menstrual cramps, sometimes so bad I couldn't stand. With severing of the spinal cord I lost that nightmare of pain and only have a distant ache occasionally. It is good being free of the pain and nausea; doctors (male) were quite useless, some clearly didn't think it was that bad. In fact it was so unpleasant that if I had the choice of being able-bodied and having that pain back I would choose to remain paraplegic. Another immediate advantage was that during rehabilitation I became strong through gradual structured exercises. When 'able-bodied' I was weak and asthmatic. I still have the asthma but I now have muscles and strength, I was even taught to swim without bother. I still feel slightly resentful that I could only get this strength when paraplegic, my previous PE teachers had no idea of these techniques.

In the last few years I find I'm afraid of further disability, I've become conscious of my good fortune in having a non-progressive disability. I'm afraid of additional injury or disease, and I'm very aware that my hands and arms are my vital tools, without them I become dependent on someone else to get me in and out of bed, etc. I fear even as much as a broken finger because of the loss of independence it would cause me. Sometimes I feel as if this could become a real phobia. I also worry about disability in my mate, that if she were ill or injured we might be separated, but was reassured to hear of a paraplegic wife who cares for her disabled husband, and now I feel I would be able to cope too.

JILL

Jill, who is blind, is 40 years old, married, with one daughter and lives in Westcliff-on-Sea, Essex. She is the public relations officer for the National Federation of the Blind and secretary of her local branch. She is also chairperson of the Southend Federation for the Handicapped, a co-ordinating organisation of thirty-two different groups. Since going blind she has learned to swim, to horse ride and she goes dancing. She is a member of the United Reform Church and recently took part in a special service for the blind, reading the lesson from braille. She broadcasts on the 'In Touch' programme on Radio 4 and has appeared in many radio and television programmes on the work of the National Federation of the Blind. Jill tape-recorded her contribution.

I was born fully sighted, but on my first birthday developed measles, followed by pneumonia, which led to the removal of my left eye. I should have gone to a special school, but my mother did not want me to leave home, so I was allowed to go to the small local school. I was able to take part in all the same activities as my fully sighted friends. When I left school I went to Southend Technical College where I obtained City and Guilds Certificates in hotel and catering subjects and eventually became director's cook for a large company.

During my nine years at college and work, I was a normal teenager, taking part in activities, such as dancing, sailing, going to the cinemas and theatres and mixing with boys. I met my husband, Michael, when I was eighteen and saved up for five years to buy our house before getting married. On the eve of our wedding, my right eye went a bit bleary, so my father called our doctor who said it was nerves and that it would be better in the morning. That day was to be a landmark in my life. I awoke to a bright, sunny morning and opened the eighty-six wedding day cards that had been sent to me. After breakfast with my parents I caught the bus to the hairdressers and then returned home to get ready for the wedding. My own dressing table had already been taken to our new house so I changed in my bedroom without being able to look at myself in the mirror. Before I had a chance to go into my Mother's room and have a look at myself, the photographer had called me into the garden for photographs and, because of the lack of time, I never returned indoors to look at myself in the mirror and so I never actually saw myself as a bride. As I walked down the aisle to the altar, I can remember seeing many friendly faces of people I had known for many years. After the wedding, we came out into the bright sunshine and I was still able to look around and see all my friends and relatives. Then we left for our reception and it was as we went into the hotel that the change of light started to make my eye go funny again. For the next few minutes I was very muzzy and I had a pain starting over the top of my eye. My husband led me to the table where we had to pose for a mock photograph cutting the cake and it was as we finished that my eye went completely. We started our meal and I didn't tell anybody but as we finished the first course, I began to feel sick and so my mother took me out to the toilet where I was sick and the pain over my eye got much worse. I told her that I didn't want anyone to know and so I returned to the table and carried on with the meal and then with the wedding reception. After a couple of dances, my eye was hurting so much that we thought we perhaps ought to leave early to go down to Eastbourne where we were to spend a week's honeymoon, hoping that my eye would be better again by the next morning as the doctor had promised.

I really don't remember much about the journey. I know we were taken by car from the hotel to the station and I can remember getting on the train. It was a very crowded train and I was very conscious of the fact that everybody must have been looking at me like most people look at newly weds, and the fact that I couldn't see them looking at me was very upsetting. By the time we arrived at Eastbourne, the pain over my eye was very bad but we still kept hoping that by the morning the pain would go and I would be able to see again. It didn't. Instead it got worse and I became quite ill, so that my husband had to phone the doctor during the night and I was admitted immediately to Eastbourne Hospital with glaucoma. On arrival at the hospital, I can remember hearing the sister saying 'Oh, she has still got confetti in her hair' and this was so, because I had just been too ill to even wash or comb my hair out. My mother and father travelled down to Eastbourne the next day and, after consultation with the doctors, it was decided that I would have to have an operation to try and save my sight and I was transferred to Southend General Hospital where I had been treated since I was one year old. I spent the next three weeks in hospital, where I had the operation, but it was not successful and I remained blind.

I had never ever met a blind person and just did not know how I was going to cope with the normal things of life like getting washed and dressed and doing my housework. My first reaction was that I would not be able to do any of these things now, and after leaving hospital I returned to my parents' home to convalesce. It was during these early weeks that I began to find out that I could do things for myself and I tried to be as independent as I could. The knowledge that I would not be able to go back to work, and therefore, we would have half the income budgeted for, was an added mental strain. We decided to go back to the house that we had saved up for for five years and see how we could cope. The days seemed to go quite quickly as it used to take me such a long while just to get up, dress and wash and to do my housework. During the first year I had my daughter Jacqueline. The first reaction of doctors when they knew that a blind person was pregnant was that I should have an abortion, but after consultation with the gynaecologist, it was agreed that I should continue with the pregnancy. Just before Jacqueline was born I had asked the gynaecologist if I could go on the Pill after the birth, but he said that this would not be suitable for me with my eye condition and that it was not advisable to have more children. Although I had not yet accepted my blindness, I agreed to sterilisation. Obviously the doctors did not think that a blind person was capable of bringing up a child.

Ever since Jacqueline's birth, I have tried to prove these doctors wrong, and show that a blind person can bring up a child as well, if not better in some cases, as a sighted person. I have to be very careful not to over-protect Jacqueline but at the same time, prevent accidents from happening. Apart from the normal routine visit from the health visitor, I had no special training or help in bringing up Jacqueline. After my post-natal, my GP visited me and asked me what help I was receiving. At that time, I had not received any help at all, only from my mother and father and my husband, so he asked me if I had a home help. I didn't even know what a home help was, so he arranged for one to come in every day to help me with my work. He also arranged for a social worker for the blind to visit me. This was the first time that I had been visited by a social worker since I had been blind. I can remember it very well. I was sitting holding Jacqueline, who was then six weeks old and they asked me if I would like to learn braille or if I would like a white stick. I said that the only problem that I had was the difficulty I had to measure out Jacqueline's milk and had they got an aid that would be able to help me. They said they would find out, but it wasn't until about four years later that I found out via the 'In Touch' programme on Radio 4, that such an aid existed. By this time it was too late. With a six-week-old baby to look after and a large house to run I certainly had not got the time to learn braille, although if I had been encouraged to learn it and given the incentive, I might have started at that time, but it was not until I met another blind person three years later, who told me that you could get knitting and cookery books in braille, that I started to learn it. I was not aware at that time that you could write as well as read braille. I was not told anything about guide dogs or about rehabilitation centres. I had taught myself how to cope indoors but I had no confidence to go out. It was not until I acquired a guide dog seven years later, that I regained my confidence. It was Topsy, my black Labrador guide dog, now ten and a half years old, who gave me back all the confidence that I had lost. Although she now guides me all over the country, I still appreciate most of all that I can go out and do my shopping whenever I want to. This was something that I had missed very much when I first lost my sight, the independence to pop round to the shops. Now Topsy will find whatever shop I want. I just have to say to her 'Find the butchers or greengrocers' and she will find it.

The natural things that a woman takes so very much for granted, like looking in a mirror to brush and comb her hair or to put her make-up on, or when she has got dressed to look in the mirror to see what she looks like, I still miss very much. It was the simple things of life that upset me most of all, like washing, dressing and doing my housework. One of the first mistakes I made was to clean my teeth with my husband's haircream. This was because the haircream and the toothpaste were in the same sized tubes. I very quickly learned I had got a nose and now automatically I just have to smell to check that I have the right tube. Dressing is a problem, knowing the difference between colours and now that my daughter is the same size, knowing whether they are her clothes or mine. I very seldom use make-up but I can put lipstick and powder on quite successfully. Although I go to the hairdressers on occasions, I normally wash and set my own hair. This has not created any difficulty for me since I lost my sight as I find rolling up the hair is just as easy as it was when I was sighted.

Over the years I have learned to accept practical guidance from friends when choosing and wearing clothes so that I can keep up with the fashions. Now that my daughter is fifteen, she is an excellent person to take shopping. I enjoy going round the large shops and feeling all the different types of clothes as this is how I judge the fashions. By feeling something I can usually get a pretty good idea whether it will suit me.

Although I had my home help for the first twelve years that I was blind, I have not had one for the past four years, since the cost went up. With a large house, I have to work to a method to cope with my housework. I miss being able to walk into a room, look around to see if the room is tidy or not. I have to go into the room and feel all round it and make sure that there are no cups or papers and other items left from the night before. This takes time and energy, even if the room does not need cleaning. To make sure that the whole room has been cleaned thoroughly, I have to work systematically, so I start by removing all objects from tops of sideboards, dressing tables, etc., polishing the complete piece of furniture, then replacing everything. I then start Hoovering from one side of the room to the other removing every piece of furniture which can be moved. Coping with washing was very difficult before I had a washing machine because there was no way that I could be sure that the washing was clean. In the past year I have bought an automatic washing machine which has braille markings. In the first few months I was too nervous to venture into the garden to put out my washing even though my husband had fixed a line for me from just outside the back door, but gradually I did go into the garden. Ironing has never really caused me any difficulty and right from the very beginning I always did my ironing in a spare bedroom, so that if anyone should call, or especially when Jacqueline was a baby, there was no chance of her having an accident. As soon as the doorbell or telephone rings, I just switch off the iron, come out of that room and shut the door with no danger to anyone and no inconvenience to people coming into the living room or kitchen. Although braille adaptations are available for irons, I did not know these existed for many years, so coped with using an ordinary iron, learning by touch where the pointer should be, treating it very much like a clock. I can feel quite easily with my fingers where the creases are and I remember the correct way that I was taught at school to iron a shirt or dress, etc., and work in the way that I was taught.

As I had been trained as a cook, it was very frustrating for me when I lost my sight and could no longer see when the Yorkshire Pudding had risen or the roast potatoes were cooked. I can remember the first cake I made for my Mother's birthday sank in the middle because I had not weighed the ingredients. I had always used scales that I looked at and did not know that weight scales were available. After my husband found a pair of weight scales for me, I had no problems and cake-making is easy once again. I did not know for many years that braille adaptors were available for my gas cooker and relied on the raised knobs already fitted on my cooker, but now I have braille adaptations to the regulo. Eventually I found out about a kitchen timer and now use that when cooking. While there are some gadgets to help blind cooks, most of the way that one has to operate is by using your other senses and working methodically and tidily, sorting out cupboards so that you know what is inside each tin. I once made a rice pudding with pearl barley because it had been put back into the wrong cupboard and another time when I opened a tin of pineapple instead of baked beans because it had been put on the wrong shelf. Washing up has not really created any problems for me except that I have to be told when cups or other china have stains and to prevent his happening I put a little bleach into my water once a week and soak all cups, and hope the stains have been removed. Many families stop their blind relatives from washing up in case they might break something, but this never happened in my family. Knitting was one of my hobbies before I went blind and I found I could knit better afterwards than when I was partially sighted. It was a lot easier once I had learned braille and could read knitting patterns for myself, as having to wait to have patterns read to me was very frustrating. I had always enjoyed sewing but I had never been very good at it as I was not able to see to thread the needle very easily and could not machine straight. When I entered my daughter for a fancy dress competition, when she was three, it was with some reluctance that I attempted to make her dress. With help from a friend to cut out the pattern, I completed the whole operation by myself and found that I could now machine straight and even thread the needle for myself. I taught myself to make a crepe rose and attached one hundred to Jacqueline's dress and entered her as a lively lady and was very pleased when she won first prize.

A question I am often asked when I give talks at schools is, 'What is it like being blind?' and I always reply by saying, 'It is very tiring.' I think this is more true of a woman than a man, and being a blind housewife and a mother is an added strain. The psychological effect of having been sterilised does depress me at times when I feel that I should have had the opportunity of having more children. Now that I am forty, I am sure that my feelings and attitudes are no different from any other woman who is forty, except for the limitations society imposes on me because I am blind, but not because I am a woman.

ANN

Ann Macfarlane was born in Norwich, Norfolk in 1939. She had six months' formal education before the onset of Still's disease at the age of 4 and has had over 120 operations on all joints. In 1961 she gained membership of the oldest short-hand society in the world and in 1962 began giving private tuition in shorthand and typewriting. After seven years she closed the business and found open employment as a medical secretary to a consultant physician. During ten working years, she travelled three times to British Columbia, New Zealand, Israel and Austria. She is now actively involved as honorary Secretary of the local Association for the Disabled and chairman of the Kingston branch of Arthritis Care. Ann is a member of the United Reform Church. She lives independently in a purpose-built flat with assistance from the community nursing service and help from parents and friends.

Newspapers and magazines take great delight in aiming articles specifically at the obese woman, and if the woman happens to be less than physically perfect the dart has scored a double bulls-eye, injuring further not only the disabled body but piercing the soul also. A woman is persuaded to 'sip an infusion of herbal tea three times a day', 'submit her body to cosmetic surgery', 'indulge in a holiday on a health farm', or 'peruse slimming diet cook books while enjoying a lazy weekend in bed'. While a woman is photographed in a bikini gently caressing a wheat sheaf with one arm and holding out a packet of 'slimming' biscuits with the other, a man rarely features in the 'battle of the bulge' unless he happens to have suffered a coronary or sports a paunch. A woman seems the main target, all aspects of her femininity being attacked, until she stands, or sits, feeling totally inferior, humiliated and a social outcast because of the additional centimetre lurking round her bosom, waist or thighs.

Obesity, plumpness, overweight, fatness, a surplus of flesh — call it any name you choose — dominated the first

half of my life. During my teens and early twenties I felt not
only unloved but unlovely and my status as a woman was
reduced to a minimum by a mountain of fat, definitely not
helped by the scores of people who murmured, 'You'll grow
out of it', 'You can't help it, it's because you can't move',
'You look perfectly all right to me'. They meant it kindly.
They were attempting to calm my active brain which was
attached to a body buckled by rheumatoid arthritis. I did
my best to avert their eyes from my five-foot frame surrounded by sixteen and a half stones by frequenting the hair-
dressing salon and laughing a great deal in order to convey
that my disability and weight were of no significance what-
soever. At times I would appear deaf, shutting out the
whispered, 'Don't push her wheelchair, you'll slip a disc',
'We can't take her on the outing, we'll never lift her up the
coach steps', and, 'We can't get involved, it's a pity she's
so heavy — such a drawback'. These remarks were true and
were often uttered by women whose own weight was less
than ideal but because they were active their problem was
not accentuated in the same way.

Not a little time was wasted on my part by blaming my
obesity on to drugs, institutional 'stodge' and my disability.
Immobility was a factor, as was a tendency to gluttony and
boredom due to the fact that, during those early years, I
had not learned how to utilise my time and the opportuni-
ties for disabled people in society were almost non-existent.
My femininity was draped, like an alabaster bust, in a short,
curly hairstyle and sack-like dresses. I made my own clothes
because I developed a phobia in the various maternity departments and 'outsize' clothes shops. I sat at the electric sewing
machine, operating the foot pedal with my hand, and
churned out the required number of shapeless garments, all
on the long side to hide my fat, diseased frame.

I was born into a loving family where food was prepared
to be enjoyed and where rejection of a second helping was
a rejection of love. Through a childhood spent mainly in the
company of medically qualified adults I was constantly

warned, 'Eat up your dinner because, if you don't mummy won't love you or be allowed to visit you.' As I grew older the emphasis was shifted to, 'You'll die if you don't eat', 'You must eat or your blood will deteriorate', or 'Your joints will become more deformed if you don't eat properly'. Nobody considered my feelings as a child, a young girl, a woman, or even as a person — a unique human being. Always, and because it was an effortless pleasure in a world of uncertainty, I did as I was told and, later, lived many a day regretting my obedience to authority. I not only burst out of my made-to-measure bras but out of my wheelchairs, the metal skirt guards breaking away from the main structure. I was not just a soul in torment but I was lumbered with a diseased body suffering additional physical distress. For years I was generally unwell as I stumbled from one diet to the next, with a craving to be slim. The fact that I would never have a body beautiful did not upset me but I longed for a few of the attributes of femininity and especially to clothe myself attractively.

A day arrived which was to transform my life. It started out as an ordinary day on which I had to travel to London for a routine check-up and when I entered the consulting room, I was greeted by a young doctor whom I had never seen before and whom I was never to see again but to whom I owe a substantial debt. 'You look pretty fed up,' he remarked. 'I'm tired of always feeling unwell,' I muttered. 'I'm sure it's because I'm so fat.' He asked me a few questions and said he could understand my attitude when I had had so many years of hospitalisation and surgery. 'You wait there, I've got just the diet for you.' He bounded out through the door and returned half an hour later holding out a bottle containing vitamin pills. 'Take these daily, they should do the trick.' 'Where's the diet sheet?' I enquired. 'Diet sheet?' he echoed, 'You can't lose weight and eat.' He summoned his nurse to wheel me from the room.

The doctor had not mentioned blood disorder or dying if I did not pamper my already gross body with food and I returned home to convince my family that I had to starve in order to survive. I reckoned I was about to launch out on a discovery of myself as an individual but, on that momentous day, I had no idea of the far-reaching consequences of that anonymous doctor's advice.

Not a morsel of food passed my lips for five months. I would have fainted on many occasions if I had not been blessed with a permanent seat. I spent hours counting and recounting my minute calorie intake each day, learning about carbohydrate and fat units, and flooding my mind with dietetic information while depriving my body of steak and fresh cream meringues. As the months passed and my gigantic proportions dwindled, I emerged as a butterfly from a chrysalis. I became truly happy, confident, daring. At the end of three years I had attained slightly below normal weight and my whole eating pattern had changed. Because I, personally, felt better without it, I ate little meat and, fortunately, really enjoyed vegetables, fruits and cheeses.

In *Fat is a Feminist Issue*, Susie Orbach suggests 'that women fear being thin . . . fat has its purposes and advantages. After an initial joyful experience of seeing themselves thin they contact feelings and ideas associated with thinness that make a woman feel cold and ungiving, angular and self-involved; admired to the point of having expectations laid on them.' The writer goes on to say that 'they feel there are no longer any excuses for the difficulties they face in their lives' and 'that when they are thin they will have no room to feel blue, and that no one will see their neediness'.

Perhaps, after all, I was hiding behind my fat in order to avoid work and social contact because of my disability. People would think my condition had improved with my 'new look' and my appearance would command less attention and sympathy. For me each day had new meaning and I was more aware of everything around me and within me. Of course I still had 'off' days and felt misunderstood but, to compensate, I enjoyed the advantage of a slight increase in energy and gained confidence to pursue ambitions. People took me more seriously and, although my disfigured body faced them square on, they appeared to accept my disability more easily, making it less of an excuse to help me, the secondary issue of fat now being discarded.

In an article I read recently, a woman in her sixties believes that 'plump can be pretty' and 'big can be beautiful' and a photograph proves her to be smart, immaculately-groomed and attractive, standing poised and relaxed in a tailored dress. That lady would be hard put to it to relate her 'outsize' story to a diseased figure. A disabled woman often does not have the financial resources for good grooming and tailored clothes. As for poise — watch a fat disabled woman getting into a wheelchair, climbing stairs on crutches or struggling into a car.

Over the years since I lost my surplus stones I have achieved numerous ambitions and goals whilst experiencing a deterioration in my physical condition. It is now more difficult to perform physical tasks in the home, more effort is required to surmount the physical barriers such as transferring from crutches to wheelchair, steering the wheelchair, mounting steps and getting into a car. Thinness has not made it less painful and awkward to dress and apply make-up, less exhausting to have my hair shampooed and styled, but once the physical effort is over I feel better, confident, and at ease with disease. My ability to deal with the emotional barriers as a disabled woman in a society where the male, albeit to a somewhat lesser degree, is still classed as the superior being, has been strengthened. I have a great love for life despite disability and the ongoing burden of mountainous fat would have stifled it, even ended it. I have a 'seen' disability, but both male and female, from every walk of life, respond to me in a far more positive way because the disability is manageable, whereas in my gross state they tolerated me at arms' length for fear that they would become involved with the problem of assisting my overweight body. They saw only the flesh and little of the spirit.

KAY

Kay, who is 46, lives in Newcastle-upon-Tyne. She is married
with three grown-up sons. She has had multiple sclerosis
since just after the birth of her first son. Before her marriage
she worked as a display artist in a departmental store. When
her children were young and she was confined to the house,
she designed and made a large variety of toys, which carried
the label 'Kay Crafts'. She was secretary of the Newcastle
Disablement Income Group.

When we were first married, I felt that I was a prized and
treasured girl. My husband had saved, and bought a house to
start our married life. He thought I should give up my job
once our wedding was arranged and just look after our home
once we were married. Eventually, in two years' time, I was
looking after our first baby as well, who I breast-fed for nine
months. Following this I found that I was unable to walk
steadily, and my doctor said it must be calcium deficiency
and prescribed some tablets. It cleared up in a fairly short
time. In another two years I had our second son and once
again took calcium tablets, having had a slight numbness in
my hands. Our third son was born after four more years
and I was with a different doctor, as the previous one died.
I asked if I should be taking calcium pills as before, but he
said, 'Oh no. there should be no need for that.' Obviously
he thought something else must have been responsible for the
trouble. Unfortunately, I had to have a breast abcess lanced
two months after this baby's birth. This is when everything changed dramatically. My condition deteriorated, and
I saw a specialist. He diagnosed multiple sclerosis, but told
me that I was suffering from neuritis. My GP was informed of
the diagnosis and passed the news on to my husband. He
was advised to tell me when he felt the time was right. I
had put two and two together myself and tried my best to
get my doctor to admit the truth. I told him that I was
having speech difficulties, thinking, 'Now he has to say what

it is', but neuritis sometimes did have that effect. It was not until I had two wisdom teeth removed in hospital, that a doctor on weekend duty, not realising that he was not supposed to mention it, blithely asked how long I had had multiple sclerosis. I just burst out laughing, 'I knew. I knew that was it.'

I regarded the third baby as being a consolation prize. I was confined to the house for three years, relying on friends to take him out. I was unable to walk any distance with his pushchair, and was then provided with a three-wheeled invalid car, so I could once again do my own shopping. But I felt that was such an obvious sign that I was a disabled person. I appreciated it of course, but I could not take my three-year-old son with me, as I had taken the other two individually on the back of my bike. It was not the same pleasure looking after a baby, and two older children, when you are disabled. I was not able to go out anywhere with them, with the baby still in his pram. I don't know how they felt, or even feel now, having their mum in a wheelchair. I have discussed their behaviour with other mothers whose children are the same age, and they just say that it is just their age. All teenagers go through the same stages and can be even more of a nuisance. Our boys are most unhelpful, which means an even greater load falls on my husband's shoulders. This does cause quite a lot of argument and I can only hope that things will improve when they are older.

The eldest found other accommodation as soon as he came of age, and just comes back at odd times. None of them did very well at school. Art was the best subject for them all and the eldest studied photography for three years in Bournemouth. He is now trying to find a job. Then the one next to him left school intending to go back after a year to sit some 'A' level exams, again. He worked in an office, on probation for a year, then after eighteen months gave it up, feeling it was not the right job for him and he is now unemployed. Our youngest son left school as soon as possible, after sitting his 'O' level exams and has not yet worked.

My husband is now unemployed. He was a salesman, and a very good one at that. Since we married he changed the firm he worked for only once and, of course, this was because of my illness. It is distressing to realise how well he would have done if it had not been for me. He couldn't take a job that would have meant that he would be away from home even for one night. He was made redundant last June and there is very little chance of getting another job when you are over 50 as he is now. I feel horribly responsible, being the one he was determined to provide for, but not intending to end up in this situation as a result.

I have a great feeling of inadequacy when it comes to helping him and the boys. How much more could I, and would I, have done, if I had not been disabled? I think I failed miserably training the boys, perhaps because there were too many other things occupying my mind. You cannot just carry on doing what you intended to do, when your life is changed completely. The boys have not been nearly as close to me as I would have liked, and I don't know what might be causing this division. Could it be that I was different from their friends' mothers? Is it just that I haven't said the right thing at the right time?

When our youngest was nine, the Government provided me with an adapted car with hand controls. This was a wonderful help, as long as there was someone to put the wheelchair into the car boot when I set off, and take it out when I arrived at my destination. This car came to the end of its economic life last year, and how I miss it. I feel imprisoned in my own home. On occasions now, my youngest son, now sixteen, pushes me out in my wheelchair and we can do shopping. I do go out once a week with my husband, to do some shopping and have coffee in the town, or to do local shopping, but for the rest of the time I just carry on doing the same repetitive jobs. I used to have a great feeling of satisfaction when I did any cooking but I'm afraid I don't do so much of that now. I can't work nearly as quickly as I did at one time and it takes me far

longer to do such a small amount. My husband doesn't seem
to understand that I enjoy it, and just says I spend far too
much time in the kitchen. When there are so many things
that you are unable to do, it is essential, I feel, to do something that satisfies you. This is when I feel sorry for my
husband as he tries to understand, and certainly does all he
can to arrange outings for me. But I am denied any freedom
of choice. You cannot just decide 'I'll go to so and so today'
or 'I'll go and see such and such a person'. You are dependent on someone else's help whenever you go out.

My husband and I have benefited from the Chronically
Sick and Disabled Persons' Act, which obliges local authorities to provide certain services for disabled people. The first
house we bought was quite unsuitable for me, and under this
Act our local authority would have provided a bathroom on
the ground floor, if there had been room. So we began the
search for another house, in the same area, with room to
make the necessary change. We were lucky as such a house
did come on the market, but it was in a very bad state of
repair and needed a lot of money to be spent on it. There was
a utility room just beyond the kitchen which was ideal for
conversion into a bathroom, plus a sitting room, living
room, a dining room which would be an ideal double bedroom, and a kitchen all on the ground floor without one step.
So we decided that this was for us and agreed to pay the
asking price. The Social Services department went ahead
with the bathroom, very soon after we bought the house, and
since then have fitted the kitchen out with everything at the
right level for me, with a split level cooker, and a ramp down
to the back garden. Unfortunately my condition has deteriorated somewhat since the bathroom fittings were installed
and I can no longer get in and out of the bath myself. This
is something that really upsets me. My occupational therapist was very good and got me an auto-lift installed, and some
rails beside the lavatory, which are now essential. Taking a
bath is an entirely different procedure now. It is no longer
a personal, feminine, pleasure. The bathroom looks more

like a shipyard. I still need my husband's help, not lifting me now, but operating the lift, and I still find it rather humiliating. Not being able to do my job as a housewife has been most irritating. We did get help from the council for this, but their home helps are so variable. Some are excellent workers and are most pleasant, but there are others who will disappear upstairs, where they know you can't follow, and please themselves what they do.

Sitting in a wheelchair permanently has a very bad effect on my state of mind, and also on my clothing. Every sweater I wear has a hole in the top of the lefthand sleeve by the metal screw on the back of the chair. Clothing is important to most women and more so, I think, to those who are disabled. I cannot wear shoes now, as my feet were swollen as a result of the side-effects of cortisone injections. I was on a course which went on far too long. I thought it was doing me good, but I think my doctor should have known better. I now depend on an old pair of sandals for winter and summer. I feel cold even in warm weather and always need the heating on in the house, with an electric over-blanket left switched on every night. I wear warm trousers all the year round, which is not the most feminine of outfits. The major aim of the Disablement Income Group (DIG) is to have a comprehensive allowance paid to cover the extra costs of disabled living. I would certainly be relieved if this meant that I would not be such a burden on my hard-working loving husband.

I love my husband dearly and we have managed to keep a good sexual relationship. All the roads in our suburb have been holding street parties since Jubilee year. I enjoy these especially as I can take part in them. This year a very good jazz band came round, on a lorry, stopping and playing for a while at each party and those who wanted to went onto the road to dance. My husband and I used to love this kind of music and he asked one of our neighbours to dance with him. I tried my best not to be affected, but I'm afraid I was very jealous. I always enjoyed dancing with him, and to see him enjoying dancing with another woman was just too much. I also love my three boys dearly and I have had occasional glimpses of a similar feeling being returned. My greatest pleasure now would be for my husband and three sons to be able to get jobs which would give them good wages and fulfilment.

FRANKIE

Frankie, who is 50 years old, suffered an attack of polio when she was 27, married, with a little girl of 5. She was in an iron lung at first, but eventually became an out-patient at Stanmore Orthopaedic Hospital for eighteen months. She was left severely disabled, in layman's terms about 80 per cent disabled, although this has no bearing on her general health or life expectancy, which are both good. However, she is completely dependent on other people for getting up and dressed and for getting out and about. Within these limitations she leads a busy life, having worked as a telephone canvasser and she now gives weekly cookery lessons. She has travelled to Glasgow and Nottingham to talk to the British Association of Social Workers about physical disability and she gave evidence to the Snowden Committee on the Integration of the Disabled.

My husband, for whom I cared deeply, was called Leo, my daughter was named Gay, and my one aim in life was to make a comfortable, happy home for them — one they would want to come home to and bring their friends. I struggled desperately to be the same wife and mother to them that I would have been had I not had polio. I had to play my role, I never could bear the thought of being a person for whom everything has to be done or just an object of pity. This was not only with regard to Leo and Gay but with all my relationships, which then, as now, had to be on equal terms for me.

I have learnt to accept different kinds of help from different people, in fact letting them help in whichever way they prefer, whether it is what I require at the time or not. I try to ask the ones who like shopping to do just that. I have certain friends who are happy taking me out so I leave that to them and others prefer to help with jobs around the house. It is a bit tough if you need to go somewhere and the only one available is the person who likes tidying cupboards. But by and large it seems to even itself out. I have also made quite a study of human nature and I try very hard not to overload any one person, if I can possibly help it. I do try to protect those that I live with from being overloaded, which is not always possible because when all the family friends and voluntary or paid helpers have gone it falls, once again, on those that live with me, and it is tough make no mistake!

What can I do for all these people in return? My main talent is cooking and I have developed quite an extensive knowledge of the subject. I find this is very useful to all my friends. Sometimes, if I have enough help, I can make things for people when they have a particular need for it; the telephone rings constantly for advice and for recipes.

Another talent I have is for sorting out my problems, which have at times been enormous. We had one period when my husband was having a nervous breakdown, my mother had had a stroke and was living with us and I was flat on my back unable to move with two slipped discs! I have had to look into things so deeply that I have emerged from it with a mind that is quite well equipped to help others see their own problems more clearly.

My husband suffered from very long periods of depression, which meant that it was really difficult for us to have much social life. Booking ahead was impossible, driving and parking in the centre of London was yet another problem, so we spent most of our time at home or with a few friends locally. The time when Leo came home from business was the highlight of my day and everything revolved around the meal I had prepared for him, but I had to find some way to occupy myself in the daytime so that I wouldn't be so dependent on visitors. I was also desperate to make some contribution to our finances however small it might be.

I did the only thing I could do lying down and that was to work on the telephone as a telephone canvasser. The work was boring and after a long period of it, became soul-destroying, but I didn't care, I was so thrilled to be working at all, and I had the evenings with Leo to look forward to.

In October 1976 I received the catastrophic blow of all time. Leo suffered a fatal heart attack at the age of fifty-four. At forty-six I now had to face life as a disabled widow. How I was going to cope with this lot I just could not imagine. By this time Gay was married and had very little need of me except, of course, for the usual things that Mums try to do for their married daughters, those that were physically possible for me to do I mean, which shortens the list anyway; which could hardly be enough to keep me going. My whole purpose in life had gone. What was I to exist for? So much time and thought had gone into trying to keep Leo on an even keel that I could not imagine how I was to live without it. Quite frankly I didn't want to continue living. I lay on the bed having no reason to get up, and not wanting to anyway, until I became very uncomfortable. When I did get up to visit the loo, movement seemed to be getting more difficult and I suddenly realised that if I didn't start moving about regularly again I would soon be bed-ridden and lose whatever mobility I had. I became quite panicky about it because I had climbed those same hurdles in the past, trying to regain muscle power, and had found it horrendous. I had no choice but to get up and move about, for the alternatives were too horrible to contemplate.

I was left with a very nice house in not too good a state of repair and a lot of financial complications, which really meant that I was not too well-off. Apart from knowing that

the house needed decorating I was extremely happy in it
and was quite terrified at the thought of having to move
from it. It had taken me years of struggle with the local
council to get it altered to suit my disability, and now,
was all that effort to go to waste? Would I still be able to
afford to live in it? One of my greatest assets besides the
house is a very caring family and a quite remarkably supportive, large circle of friends. Little did they know just how
caring and supportive they were to be! Financially, for some
time I managed with all the benefits I was entitled to, plus
some help from the family. Everyone was advising me to
sell the house because it needed so much doing to it, and
because I had four bedrooms which seemed ridiculous for
me alone. Every time it was mentioned I burst into floods of
tears. I knew I didn't want to live alone and it was always
in the back of my mind that were I to suffer any more
periods of immobility, for one reason or another, at least
I could let a couple of rooms. This would provide me with
some company and a little life in the house besides bringing
in some money. I always saw the house as a possible source
of revenue.

In the meantime a few friends got together and suggested
that I hold a class in my own kitchen to teach them some
slightly more adventurous cooking, things suitable for enter-
taining and a little above average, I would even be able to
extend myself. I quite liked that idea. Anything to give me
something to do. I hated the fact that no one was leaving
the house in the morning or coming home at the evening;
I hated having no one to cook for. The evenings seemed
endless, I thought I would go quite mad with the thought
of having to live like this for years to come. I soon realised
that now the daytime had to be the best and that I must
avail myself of all the kind offers I was getting from my
friends to go out. Certainly I didn't want to spend any more
time on the telephone canvassing. More than anything I
needed a purpose, a complete new daily routine. I couldn't
live waiting for people to take me out.

About this time a little miracle took place. An old friend of mine asked me if I would like to have her seventeen-year-old son, Howard, come and live with me, owing to the fact that they had a lot of problems at home. I jumped at the idea and it was no sooner said than done! Up until then I'd felt I had been cut off in the midst of life. At forty-six I knew I still had a lot to give. Why not let Howard benefit from all these circumstances and turn what could have been misery for all concerned into a happy, viable situation, giving both of us just what we needed. I am quite sure that Howard had no idea of the enormity of what he was undertaking in living with someone who is so dependent on others, but in return I have bent over backwards to see that he benefits in every possible way and I treat him exactly as I did Gay. It seems to have worked extremely well, the fact is that two years have passed, he is still here and we are the best of friends.

With Howard's help and that of a very dear friend I was able to start the cookery classes on one day a week and they have proved very successful. A lot of work goes into planning the lessons; there is the timing to work out and recipes to get photo-copied, etc., to say nothing of the shopping lists and the food preparation on the day before. I do some day courses and some evening ones. The people who come to the day courses are given a little snack lunch, which also has to be prepared beforehand. I continue to swear that every time is the last for lunch but it seems to be so much a part of the enjoyment that I haven't the heart to stop doing it.

Things were running pretty smoothly now and we soon decided to let another couple of rooms. With inflation it was necessary anyway. By this time I was running a pretty busy household, cooking a meal for three of us every night and doing the weekly cookery lesson. This makes me a far more valued, regular customer to the smaller shop-keepers that I have to buy from, simply because they can still deliver. It also keeps me pretty occupied but still leaves me some free time, providing we plan it well enough, to go out and about with my friends. I am able to go to the theatre, to concerts and restaurants as often as one can afford. I have quite a few single women friends of my own age, though when I first became widowed I felt rather isolated from them because they were more able to look for new husbands than I was. I was proved wrong because some of them were friends of long standing and they seemed to make time for me as well. Two friends took me on the Jetfoil to Dieppe for the weekend and what a memorable weekend it was too! Physically I am better than ever because I go out so regularly. No more fighting to regain lost muscle power, I just don't allow myself to lose it.

Life is pretty hectic most of the time. The house is often teeming with people. Perhaps that is why when it goes quiet it really does go quiet — so terribly still.

MURIEL

Muriel, who is in her 50s, lives alone in Newcastle-upon-Tyne. She has been wheelchairbound for over ten years with severe rheumatoid arthritis. She has a specially adapted flat with many aids, but nevertheless, despite her badly twisted hands, before her husband went into hospital, she was changing the bed linen at least once daily and often during the night, due to his incontinence. Now that he is hospitalised she visits daily and washes all his clothes. She has actually spent the greater part of her adult life looking after first her mother, then her husband.

Her contribution was tape-recorded by Anna Briggs.

My mother had a stroke when she was forty-eight which left her paralysed down one side. In those days, there were no home helps, no auxiliaries to come out and give you a hand to wash and dress her and you had all the washing to do yourself. There were practically no social services and you were expected to look after her, even though *you* were disabled. It was a daughter's duty. At the time I already had rhematoid arthritis and although I could walk around I could only do it with great difficulty. The amount of washing I had to do was quite considerable, and in those days again there weren't things like automatic washing machines, even if you had the money, which we didn't. My mother had worked but there wasn't a great deal in the way of social benefits as there are today, so that we had very little to provide all the necessaries. A washing machine wasn't considered necessary. You were supposed to wash sheets and get them dried and put them on the bed, that was the normal way. So I got absolutely exhausted, I went down to just under six stones in weight, because I looked after her. She was my mother and there was no question of trying to put her away. Even if I had wanted to put her into care, at that time there was no way you could do it, it was a daughter's duty to look after her parents. A daughter didn't have a life of her own. When she died I got a job, not anything very glamorous but at least I did earn my own living, and this was the great thing. I think people don't realise the amount of dignity you get out of having a wage packet. I can remember getting a job in old money for £3 a week, and I had been getting £2.17s.6d. a week dole, so I was working for less than half a crown a week, but it was *my* money. *I'd* worked for it. One of the things I find very irritating is that people tend to look at you as you are now, in a chair, and they think that you've always lived on the state, but that's not true, there's an awful lot of disabled people who have worked, and worked very hard. We've worked at jobs that nobody else would take, low-paid, dirty, unpleasant jobs. There seems to be two standards of living, one for the non-disabled and one for the disabled, and the thing is, what is for the disabled will do, but if you're not disabled, it won't do for you. People seem to be surprised that you have a standard, because perhaps you can't get washed yourself, so they think it doesn't really matter, but I like my dignity, I want to be as clean and as smart as anybody else, and I find it very irritating. I'm only human, I haven't a lot going for me, but what I've got I like to make the most of, like every woman. They seem to think that because you're disabled you have no feelings, no emotions, nothing, you're just like a robot.

I met my husband at a club for disabled people, and this is another thing, that disabled people don't have a great deal of social life. People tend to think that they can put all the disabled together. Now you can put a group of doctors or a group of nurses or any kind of people together, it doesn't mean to say that because they've got one profession they're all going to get on together, and it's the same with disabled people, we're people first and disabled second. So that's how I met my husband. He has now unfortunately developed senile dementia, which is a very difficult disability to cope with for those who have to look after them. He became doubly incontinent, very confused, and rather difficult to deal with. If he smoked he would drop lighted matches about and set the place on fire, so he had to be taken into care eighteen months ago, but I go and see him every day. He'd had paralysis when he was a little boy, so he's got a double handicap now.

When we got married it was a dirty joke. This is what I mean about they don't think you have the same emotions, the same desires or worries, as able-bodied people. You fall in love, you love somebody, you don't see the disability in them, you just see the person. You don't see the crutches, or sticks, or calipers, or wheelchairs, you see a man, and like most women when they meet a man they like, you only see the good points in them. They would say to you, 'What are you getting married *for*?' in a rather sleazy, dirty attitude. The kinds of questions that strangers would ask, people that you didn't know very well — 'What will you do if you have a family?' 'What sort of a sex life will you have?' — I wouldn't think that they'd ask able-bodied couples things like that, and my husband's rather shy, he found it very distressing. I found it just annoying, your whole life is public, you haven't to have any privacy, they like to know every little detail of your life.

As a woman, naturally I wanted children, but we made the decision not to because we didn't think it would be fair on the child. But we still had emotional feelings, we still gave each other strength and companionship, and a lot of people don't understand that, they think that you have got to be sort of producing and it wasn't quite nice for disabled people to produce children. Well that's up to the disabled person, if they want to go ahead and have a family it's got nothing to do with anybody else. What I had wasn't hereditary but there's more to children than having a baby. You see if we'd had children we both would have liked to take them to the country and shown them wild flowers, wild life, taken them to the coast and had picnics, take them bathing, do all the normal things that families do. Love by itself isn't enough for a child, it's got to have experiences, it's got to learn and to grow emotionally as well as physically and that would have been impossible with us. So in a way, we loved our children too much to have them. We sacrificed our children, so that although they wouldn't have a future they weren't going to have a rotten future with two disabled parents hanging round their neck. I don't think you have children to comfort you in your old age, yes of course, you expect that when you have children and you have a good relationship then you want them to come to you when you're ill or you're getting a bit old and you need some moral support, but you don't have them to sacrifice the children to your life, that isn't what having children is about, I don't think it is. I think that partly comes from my experience looking after my mother and when I've looked around and seen people, women, who because they've been the only daughter, or they've been the daughter who isn't married they are expected to sacrifice their lives to look after parents and sometimes the parents live so long because they're well looked after. By the time they die the daughters are so worn out there's no life left for them, and this is wrong, you don't have families for that, or I don't think you should. What is the alternative — and really women are blackmailed? As a woman I feel that I'm even now emotionally blackmailed sometimes into doing something that's really beyond my strength but I've still got to find the strength from somewhere to do it. Things like going to see my husband, I go up every day, he's dependent on me, he gets very distressed if I don't go up. People still think that I should go on giving myself, even though he isn't at home. It isn't that I don't want to give of myself, but we can all only give so much, and we do have a life, and so often we have to suppress our own feelings, I think, and this is where I think we're emotionally blackmailed because in a way I think we're brainwashed into thinking we should do it.

When I had to give up work, it was after my pelvis twisted and it left me with one leg shorter than the other, the doctor said I would never walk again and they wanted me to go into care. I felt dreadful when I had to give up work, it was the most shattering experience I had had, because going out to work, you felt part of society, you were contributing, you were earning your own money. You also had your friends that you went to work with, and then suddenly you were cut off, you were in the house alone. Also of course financially you were worse off. You were lonely, you felt useless, on the scrap heap, finished, and it really was a very bad time. It wasn't only the idea that you could no longer work, it was the worry of what was going to happen to you, I wasn't married, had no family, no relations. What was going to happen to me? I was frightened. I thought it was the end of the world. Of course it wasn't, that's one thing about disablement, you do learn that you have a crisis but come through it, and so you seem to stagger from crisis to crisis, but you do get through. It is important for women to be able to work, I know you're needed when you're a housewife and at home, but you also have a social need, you want to be out and part of life, because life goes over very quickly and you want to mix with your own generation, there's something that you don't get at home that you get outside at work.

I married about five years after that, and slowly I got back on to my feet. I had one leg shorter than the other but I could get around. We were married for about seven or eight years when I became ill and then it was just impossible for me to think of working again. When I got out of bed, both legs had just gone, and again, you see, I thought that was the end of the world because nobody thinks they can live from a wheelchair, but by gum you can, you can do a lot from a wheelchair. I think there's a great lack of counselling for people who become disabled and have to go into wheelchairs, I don't mean people who just have a limp, I mean really disabled people. Up to a point of course, you have to get through on your own, it's your own personal decision which way you take it, but I think if only there was somebody who would understand the frustrations, the way you feel, your anger, your bad temper, your aggression. There's nothing worse than somebody who's fit and healthy slapping you on the back and saying 'You'll cope' and you look at them and think 'What the hell do they know about it, they're walking around!' but you can take it from somebody else who's in a chair because they've gone through it and they know.

I think disabled people are not used enough. I think that many disabled people do become lethargic, lazy, couldn't care less, and it is not always their fault. They become this way because so often it is quicker for the able-bodied to push them out of the way, to push a wheelchair along, to do things for us, till you come to a point where no matter how strong-willed you are, you give up, you say 'Let them get on with it'. But I think there is a great source of energy, not really physical energy, but mental energy that isn't being tapped, and I think we could relieve able-bodied people by this energy, because we *could* do counselling, we *could* understand. We understand the way disabled people think. So often you get committees, you get all these people who, I know it sounds dreadful, they think they are doing so much good, but they never stop and think 'Right, what do the disabled themselves think?' They go ahead with all these magnificent plans, and of course as far as we're concerned it's a right mess-up, and then when you say something, they get really very hurt that you are criticising all their hard work, which I can understand, but if only they would have stopped first and said 'Let's consult the disabled' because we're not all idiots! I don't think things are changing, not a lot, there are some areas where it's a bit better, but I still find the tendency for a lot of people to shut the disabled out, or what is just as insulting, like the statutory woman, have a disabled person on sufferance, but they don't really want to know what you think, they just want you there to make the numbers up and just be seen.

Clothing is getting to be quite a problem for me because as my physical condition gets worse I am finding it rather difficult to manoeuvre clothes. It does annoy me when a well-meaning occupational therapist says, 'Well, get a size bigger.' I don't want to look like something that's come off a dustcart. I want my clothes to fit, it's important to me to look nice, as nice as I can. I'm not going to sit around looking like something that's come up from a jumble sale. Why should I? Would any other woman? The electric wheelchair improves things — one of the advantages of shopping with the chair is that there's nobody behind me when I choose what I want. There's none of this 'What does she want, what colour does she want?' That happens when you're being pushed around by someone. This is a common complaint amongst disabled people in chairs. They always say the assistant *will* ask the person who's doing the pushing, as thought you were a halfwit. I find it marvellous that I can go into a shop and buy a pair of tights for 25p or a three-piece suit for £25 and nobody knows but me how much it cost, where I got it from, and this is great. It gives you such a great feeling it's just between you and the shop, how much you paid for it. Before that, somebody knew, and no matter how good a friend you are, you don't always want them to know how much you pay for all the things you buy. It's your privilege to tell them or not to tell them, but when they're standing there and they know exactly what you've spent, this is part of the thing that I don't like. Especially for disabled women, it's just not expected that you want any sort of privacy in your life at all. The home help goes to the post office, she gets your money, she takes your rent, so she knows how much you've got coming in and how much rent you pay, it isn't really that I want to be secretive, but I do want just that little bit that somebody doesn't know about. It's private and it's part of me — it's like living in a goldfish bowl that everybody can see and know what you're doing. I think we all need to have that little bit of ourselves that's shut away, that nobody else knows about.

I get a bit despondent with the way things are, and they don't seem to be getting any better. I think that one of the things I would like to see changing is the attitude to aids which are very important for disabled people. The powers-that-be, like the local authority, have a set idea of what there is. They haven't got a wide enough horizon. With the silicon chip coming there are going to be many more so-called luxury goods but they're going to be fantastic for disabled people. But local authorities don't want to know because they are luxury goods that only rich women should have. I wonder if it would be the same if I was a man. I need a different kind of telephone in the bedroom but if I had it put in, it would cost me £10 per quarter more because it's a luxury! The very fact that it is a necessity for me doesn't come into it, it's a luxury. I'm fortunate I suppose because I've got a dishwasher, not because they're a luxury but because my hands are too bad to wash dishes. And people say, 'Oh, fancy you having a dishwasher' and 'Aren't you lucky, I can't afford one'. And I know it's not very nice but I say

'Tell you what, give me your hands and you can have my dishwasher' and they take offence, but why should they if I'm not supposed to take offence at being told that I've got luxuries? People still expect you to live on a lower level and if you're a disabled woman, somehow you're supposed to cope, you're not supposed to get tired, bad-tempered or frustrated or want to throw something through the window. You're not supposed to do it, you're a woman, and that's your job, and you're supposed to have some inner strength and you can go on and on and on.

I think disabled men get supported more, I know by experience, I've seen men who were not half as disabled as a lot of women and my goodness they're run after hand and foot, because 'It's not nice, it takes their dignity away', that a *man* has been disabled, that a *man* has been the bread-winner and therefore it's a tragedy if he becomes disabled. If a housewife becomes disabled, she's somehow expected to carry on, it's not a tragedy. In some people's eyes it's a bigger tragedy because if a woman is taken out of a house, that house will collapse. A man, I know you miss his money, you miss the man but let's face it, how many women have to cope on their own, not only cope on their own but cope with a disability and very often children. It's surprising how many men just can't face the fact that their wives are disabled and they just go off and leave them with kids and all to fend for themselves. I think that's very common — I know quite a few women who've been left in the lurch just because they've become disabled, and yet I know women who have stuck to their husbands and wrecked their own health looking after severely disabled husbands and in turn the women are now really disabled themselves and they've gone on years and years and years, long after they should have given in and said 'I can no longer cope'. I tried to cope for too long quite frankly and I thought that when my husband did go away I would get my strength back but it isn't working out that way. I've spent that strength and there's no way I'm going to get it back. But you see you were his wife and you were expected to cope, as a woman that was part of being married, and to me it isn't, there should be equal shares. I don't want more shares than anybody else, but I want my share of rights, I want my share of dignity and compassion and there's not a lot of it around for women.

WYN

Wyn was born in County Durham in 1924. She studied nursing at the General Infirmary at Leeds where she qualified as a State Registered Nurse. She did midwifery training at Northampton General Hospital and the South London Hospital for Women, becoming SCM, and returned to the General Infirmary at Leeds as ward sister, then assistant sister tutor and finally night superintendent. During this time she studied for limited periods at the Royal College of Nursing in London, obtaining Ward Sister's and Nursing Administration Certificates.

After marriage she became Assistant Regional Nursing Officer, Leeds Regional Hospital Board. In 1957 she won a British Commonwealth Nurses War Memorial Fund Scholarship which enabled her to study nursing in Canada and the USA. In 1961 she had a baby daughter, Anne. Following maternity leave she returned to her position at the Leeds Regional Hospital Board. When Anne was 1 year old, she left home in her usual way to drive to work in Harrogate. She was innocently involved in a head-on car crash as a result of which she had multiple injuries including damage to the spinal cord in her neck. This resulted in her becoming a tetraplegic with complete paralysis from her neck downwards including all four limbs. In addition there was loss of sensation to all these parts so she has no control over her bladder and bowels. After three years in the Spinal Injuries Unit in Wakefield, she returned home to be cared for by her

family and the district nurses. She has continued in this way
for the past eighteen years. Although unable to return to
work she leads a very active life, lecturing on the problems of
disability to a wide range of audiences from medical staff,
nurses and physiotherapists to all kinds of public bodies. She
also does much work for the Spinal Injuries Association of
which she is vice chairman and takes an active part as a
Member of the Bradford Community Health Council.

She has written a large number of articles for various
journals on aspects of disability and has also appeared in
several BBC radio and TV programmes.

Prior to my being severely disabled I took a great pride in my
appearance. I soon learned, after my accident, that having to
rely on other people to wash me, dress me and maintain the
appearance to which I had been accustomed was, and still is,
fraught with great difficulties and frustration. The first
time I looked in a mirror after my accident I hardly recognised myself. For practical reasons I was dressed in trousers
with a pair of flat-heeled lace-up shoes. Since I had usually
worn dresses or skirts and high-heeled court shoes, my new
appearance demoralised me beyond words.

Whilst my hair had been kept clean and washed by the
nursing staff it had not been cut for about three months with
the result that this did nothing to enhance my appearance.
The nursing staff were very co-operative and they organised
a hairdresser to come to the hospital. That improved the
situation but hair remains a perennial problem. Until four
years ago visits to the hairdressers were a major operation.
Having to be lifted into and out of a car and trying to get
into salons which were often difficult from an access point
of view added to the problem. It took two people to tilt my
wheelchair back so that my hair could be washed in the
basin. After washing and setting it commonly happened that
the manhandling necessary to get me into, then out of a
car and back into my wheelchair undid all the good work
that had been done. In addition I was not independent to

choose the day and time when I could have my hair done but had to rely on the available timings of friends to transport me to the hairdresser. Bad weather in winter added to this problem often making it impossible to go at all. Now, however, the district nurses wash my hair using a hand shower whilst I am in the bath and I have a hairdresser who comes to the house. This has eliminated some of the problems but the situation limits the scope of the hairdresser and the time at which it can be done is also restricted. Thus it is frequently impossible to arrange for all these things to take place just prior to attending some functions for which I would formerly have had my hair dressed.

The clothes I had worn before my accident no longer fitted me, so I had to find clothes which were attractive and practical. I soon found that separates were more practical than dresses. Trying on 'tops' did not present too great a problem. I was of course completely unable to try on skirts in a shop and in order to do this I have to be subjected to the arduous business of being lifted from my wheelchair on to a bed, my skirt removed and the new one pulled on for me. I must then be lifted back onto the chair to see if the skirt fits and how it looks. Then the process of lifting me back on to the bed to remove the skirt and replace my own is necessary. It will be realised that to try on half a dozen skirts is an impossibly arduous task for two helpers and myself and it was common to find that no skirt I tried on was suitable. Fortunately during the last few years a friend who has good taste in choosing materials and the willingness and ability to make them up especially for me has solved many of my problems. I can rely on her to bring me samples of materials for me to make a final selection. Fortunately nowadays there are many attractive materials which are 'easy-care' and durable. The latter factor is very important as my clothes have to stand up to a great deal of wear and tear as they are regularly being pulled on and off a helpless person lying on a bed. Skirts with very long zips make for easier dressing and undressing. The greater length also means that less stress need be placed on them thus reducing the number of times I have to ask friends to replace broken zips. As I have no control over my legs nor the ability to adjust them should they be in an ungainly position, I find long skirts which conceal them to be more practical. Long skirts also have the advantage of concealing the leg drainage bag for urine and thus I wear this type of skirt for day, evening, summer and winter. I stick to a basic pattern and bring in variety by means of colour and texture. I do not find it necessary to wear flat-heeled shoes as I find that court shoes with stiletto heels have the added bonus that the heels can be made to fit behind my wheelchair footplates thus preventing the involuntary spasms in my legs from moving my feet and scraping them on the footplates or other objects. I should point out here that a small scratch or abrasion can be very difficult to heal in a person with paralysed limbs. In my own case damage to my ankle from a small abrasion has taken up to a year to heal. My appearance is even more important now that I am confined to a wheelchair as I am usually more conspicuous and also I am not independent to slip away and adjust myself if I feel that my appearance is in any way in need of this. This reduces the pleasure of going out.

I like to use some make-up even though only a minimum. My choice of lipstick container is one which I can use my teeth to remove the case and then use the trick movement of my wrist to push up the lipstick. My chin can be used to press on the top of a perfume atomiser so that I can apply some myself. A brush comb inserted into a leather strap which I can push over my hand enables me to comb my hair. After a lot of shopping around I found a beauty case which has a mirror in the lid. This is needed as most cloakroom mirrors are too high for a person in a wheelchair to be able to use them.

The female anatomy adds to the difficulties of the severely disabled woman. When I became disabled I lost control over my bladder and since then have relied on a self-retaining catheter for urine drainage. As the urethra and vagina are in close proximity to one another it is not difficult for someone inserting a new catheter to place it by accident into my vagina instead of my urethra. When this happens the catheter has to be discarded, causing delay in catheterising me and extra cost to the NHS as catheters are quite expensive items. The reverse situation has occurred when I was being treated for a vaginal infection. On that occasion a pessary was inserted into my bladder via my urethra instead of into my vagina. Tampon cartons and cotton wool swabs have also been lost by being left in my vagina. Suppositories intended for my rectum have also been inadvertently inserted into my vagina. Many people think that it is impossible for events such as this to take place but I can assure them from personal experience that it has happened. Insertion of anything into one's bladder is liable to cause infection and this is far greater when the object is not intended for that area and hence not appropriately sterilised.

Many able-bodied women find that menstruation is a nuisance. For the severely disabled woman it is a major difficulty. Firstly I have no sensation and therefore have no idea when I start to menstruate. Secondly it is impossible for me to insert a tampon or fix a sanitary pad in position myself. Thirdly I am unable to change myself. Thus once the nurses have inserted a tampon and applied a pad I must remain like this until I can be put to bed again in the evening. In order not to stain my clothes and increase the amount of washing I try to guess when I am due to menstruate and ask the nurse to insert a tampon as a precautionary measure a few days before the expected event. I also feel that the insertion of tampons is a very personal thing which since it cannot be done by myself should be done by a nurse or a female member of the family and not by my husband who in fact frequently has to do it and is quite competent at it. Once menstruation is established the nurse inserts two tampons and applies a pad. I then hope that I am adequately protected until I can be changed that evening. If I wish to go to a social engagement this adds to the complications since I have to try to find two people to lift me from wheelchair to bed, change my tampons, re-dress me and lift me back into my wheelchair. The menopause increases the difficulty if one is suffering from heavy menstrual loss and cannot change tampons. If such heavy loss is due to hormonal causes the situation can be controlled by taking hormones to stop the bleeding. With the best possible planning, however, accidents still happen and one is faced with an embarrassing situation on finding oneself lifted from a wheelchair revealing a bloodstained cushion. In turn, one's clothing proves to be soaked in blood which passes the stain on to the bedclothes on to which one is being lifted.

Men who have lost control over their bladder can in some cases use a urinal or a condom. Unfortunately a satisfactory urinal has not been produced for women. It is necessary therefore for women to use a permanent self-retaining catheter. This brings with it the danger of introducing infection, promoting calculus formation and in turn causing damage to bladder and kidneys. I have had to have three major operations on my kidneys for this reason.

No longer is it possible for me to do the household shopping or take part in any of the normal household duties. This adds to one's frustrations. It means that the family in addition to looking after the disabled person are confronted with all the household duties including shopping, cooking, laundry, etc. Domestic help is both difficult to obtain and expensive and this can add to the financial difficulties of the situation.

Psychological barriers play an important part in my life. An early example of this was six weeks after my accident when I saw my year-old daughter. My immediate reaction was to try to pick Anne up and give her a hug. The loss of power and movement in my arms made this impossible, added to which my loss of sensation prevented me from feeling her next to me. It has also been a constant source of distress to me that I have not been able to tuck Anne into bed. To see everyone else doing this is a most frustrating and depressing experience particularly when one realises that it will never be possible to do this normal human motherly task. The physical lack of awareness of contact must to some extent be set against the following gain. I have always had time to listen to any of Anne's problems and share her accounts of her doings. When our domestic help suddenly left, Anne, who was only seven years old, had to be guided verbally by me as she prepared simple meals. It was not easy to sit helplessly by, watching her cook, serve the meal, cut up my food into small pieces and even feed me with certain items of food. I found the latter most humiliating. Had it been practical, my daughter and I would have enjoyed shopping expeditions for clothes but these had to be kept to a minimum from a practical point of view.

Travelling by car is still an enjoyable experience for me as I have no recollection of the precise circumstances of my accident. However it takes two people to lift me into and out of the car and I usually end up in my wheelchair with my clothes in a state of disarray. I often feel humiliated and wish that I could independently adjust my clothes. The situation is even more degrading if there are a number of people waiting to meet me by the car and I am unable to make myself presentable.

Life is a constant struggle trying not to feel different from able-bodied people. Even the simple use of a serviette illustrates this. My serviette has to be clipped to my blouse or dress collar so that it is held in position and is thus able to protect my clothing. I try not to spill my food but the fact that my fingers are paralysed means that I am unable to hold cutlery normally. So from time to time food is spilt, and in order to save washing my clothes each time it is more practical to have my serviette clipped to my collar. This makes me feel different to other people and I object to it. Being unable to handle an ordinary teacup it often happens that someone will attempt to give me a drink from one. Now in the first place the liquid may be far too hot but once someone else is pouring it into your mouth you are unable to speak to tell them to stop. If the situation becomes really unbearable one has to attempt to withdraw one's mouth with the result that the hot liquid invariably cascades down one's chin, neck and clothes. Oddly enough the person assisting with the cup usually wonders why I have been stupid enough to do this. A similar situation can arise even if the liquid is of drinkable temperature. Someone kindly lifts the cup to my lips and pours the liquid as fast as or even faster than I can drink it, into my mouth. Eventually I am desperate to stop drinking to take a breath but the assistant does not realise this and I am unable to stop the flow of fluid in order to speak to them. In the end I am forced to stop and the liquid cascades down the front of my dress. A slight variant of the hot liquid episode is when I have on occasion been given a very hot drink from a cup or beaker using a straw or a plastic tube. All goes well at first and I suck the liquid up in the small amounts needed and then swallow it. Either to assist the process or quite unconsciously, the person holding the beaker gradually raises the height of it. Suddenly it happens that having drawn it into the drinking straw and obtained the required amount in my mouth I find that ceasing to apply suction no longer has any effect and the scalding hot liquid pours in a continuous stream from the straw into my mouth. The reason is that the beaker now has a higher liquid level than the top of the straw in my mouth. Under these conditions, once started, the flow of liquid continues to siphon from beaker to mouth without any assistance or control from me. Again the disastrous sequence of events can only be broken by my opening my mouth and thereby spilling the contents down my clothing.

The fact that I am always seated in a wheelchair with limited neck and hand movement causes me both embarrassment and difficulty. I dislike the situation in an audience when everyone else stands for some reason and I am unable to do so. Also when the audience applauds and I am unable to join in as I am unable to clap my hands together. Few people realise how difficult it is for a person in a wheelchair when a group of people stand nearby and hold a conversation in which the wheelchair person is supposed to be included. In the first place it rapidly becomes uncomfortable for me to tilt my head back all the time so that I am looking up towards them. Also it is difficult to understand, in such a situation, that the person in the wheelchair has great difficulty in hearing conversation directed at the other people several feet above one's head. Perhaps the greatest insult one feels in this type of situation is when one has been pushed into a shop to make a purchase. All too frequently the shop assistant addresses the remarks concerning the purchase, not to the purchaser in the wheelchair but to the companion pushing it.

When one member of a family is seriously disabled, the whole family is disabled. As in my case it may well mean that the family has one income instead of its former two. To me also it is very frustrating that when my husband comes in from work in the evening I cannot have a meal ready for him. Instead he has to start and prepare the evening meal. Then if I am in need of any form of attention during the night my husband has to get up and attend to me. But despite having had his night's sleep disturbed he has to go to work as usual the next day. Despite the difficulties of being a severely disabled person I think that life is still worth living. I have a loyal understanding husband. Our daughter unknowingly has brought us untold pleasure. My voluntary activities and giving lectures on the problems of disability to a wide range of people from NHS staff to voluntary organisations keeps me fully occupied and I find that I am very busy with little spare time.

DIANA — II

Diana, who is now 60, lives with her mother of 92 in London. A stroke in 1967 left her paralysed down the right side and completely unable to communicate in speech or writing. Her speech is now adequate, although halting, but she cannot write. Her difficulty with writing is not caused by the fact that her right hand is paralysed, as she had learnt to use her left hand for this function, and she can copy write efficiently. The difficulty is that although she knows what she wants to write, she is unable to recall the words she wants to use. This is the same problem as her speech and both her spoken and written language are agrammatical. Furthermore, although she can recall the word or sentence, she is unable to write it down because she cannot recall the letter shapes which go together to make up the words. Earlier Diana was unable to write single letters to dictation but this is not a problem now. However she has only a very small written vocabulary. Her contribution to this book was the result of the combined efforts of Diana, two of her 'scribes' and Margaret Freeman, LCST, Chief Speech Therapist of the Middlesex Hospital.

Diana was one of the founders of 'Action For Dysphasic Adults' and she inspired and helped to set up a network of speech clubs throughout the country and abroad. In 1978 she was awarded an MBE. Her book *Living After a Stroke* (with Barbara Paterson) was published by Souvenir Press in 1980.

By the time I was forty-seven I was, I think, successful in my career and leading a very full and active life. My work, as Manager of the Education Liaison Services for a computer company, was challenging, as the computer industry was still just developing. I was involved with several committees and had written two books and a number of articles on my subject. My social life was equally full; I loved the theatre and concerts, parties and sport. I had stood as a candidate in local government and parliamentary elections. I was independent, active and I loved to talk!

Suddenly everything was changed by a subarachnoid haemorrhage. Even when it all began, it seemed not too bad. I had surgery and remember three days of visits, laughter, cards and flowers and then I had a stroke. That time is hazy for me, but my mother and sister have a clear memory of me, paralysed down my right side and unable to speak. The doctor told them I was a hopeless case and that I was 'virtually an idiot' now. Thank God, they did not accept his verdict. My mother was convinced he was wrong; she says she could tell from my eyes that I was alert, but my lack of speech confused us all.

In the first three months I made a lot of physical recovery. My arm and leg were still paralysed, but with physiotherapy and occupational therapy, I began to walk and dress myself. I didn't feel the arm and leg were a problem, though; my lack of speech was far more worrying — all I could say was 'tonight and tonight and tonight'! No one seemed to know what to do to help and their lack of understanding made it all far worse. I have a clear memory of doctors and nurses standing near my bed talking . . . I felt left out . . . I wanted to talk. I couldn't even communicate my basic needs. They thought I was incontinent when I wet the bed but it was because I couldn't tell them when I needed to go to the lavatory. There was not even a bell or a buzzer so I could call for help.

The frustration of miscommunication was overwhelming. I lay in that bed comparing my previous competence with this new and frightening state. I have always had strong faith and I felt that through this experience, God was giving me a new goal. He was telling me to work for others who had problems and I vowed that, in every way I could, I would use my skill with speech to campaign for greater understanding of people with speech disorders. I've worked hard to keep that vow but I am still amazed at the number of people who rely on their speech, reading and writing skill in their work — such as MPs, government departments and journalists — who are ignorant of the devastating effect of speech impairment!

My mother and sister had to fight first, though. They fought and fought and fought to get me to a rehabilitation centre where I could have speech therapy. It took three applications and many letters to all sorts of influential people to get me admitted, but I was finally taken to the Wolfson Medical Rehabilitation Centre. It was there that Michael Jackson, the speech therapist, told my mother and sister what had happened to my speech. I didn't understand the explanation then, but I was delighted that at last someone understood me and knew I was *not* an idiot. It was a great relief to know that I was not the only person to ever have been like this — there were eight people like me there at the time.

It was lovely to feel safe in the hands of the speech therapist. The joy of producing even a few words and the relief of knowing I could get better is still a vivid memory for me. It was very bad speech but never mind, I could say something! At that stage, I used three phrases constantly 'it's madness!' 'wonderful' and 'but, but, but'. They may be symbolic in a sense, but in fact a speech therapist would label them as recurrent utterances, a sort of 'prop' phrase which came out more easily than the more meaningful speech I actually wanted to use. But it was progress and I was happy.

Then, all of a sudden, the Wolfson discharged me. I returned home to live mainly with my mother, sometimes with my sister Jacqueline and her husband, David. I was distressed and devastated by this sudden change and all I could do was cry. I *did* have private speech therapy twice a week at home from Joan Ellams, a speech therapist from Camden Rehabilitation Centre, but it was not enough. I knew I needed more and although the family tried constantly to help, I still felt desolate. My mother especially refused to give in although after five minutes of her work I would be tired again and weepy. The closeness of my family and friends kept me going during this time. My mother in particular continued to be an indomitable driving force; it was so typical of her to keep going even though she must have been exhausted. (She was seventy-nine when I had the stroke.) Her refusal to let me give up helped me find my own fighting spirit again; we are very similar in character. At home, alone, she would talk constantly, asking me the names of everything in the room and demanding answers. When friends came, she insisted that I should be kept in the conversation although it was hard for me to follow a lot of talking. My sister and her husband also worked hard; David, my brother-in-law, played dominoes and cards with me and even found a one-arm card-holder so I could play one-handed, even though I could only manage 'snap'.

I think it was at that time that I realised how much had changed. I knew it was not only my speech or my walking, etc., but my independent life style was in jeopardy. I was decidedly slowed down in every way. Before, I walked briskly, talked quickly and was a very active person in my work and in my social life. Many of the things I loved like the theatre, concerts and parties are no longer so pleasurable. Where I used to have boyfriends, now I have friends who are men. My periods stopped and, though I enjoy kisses and cuddles, any interest in sex disappeared too. My brain works fast but the messages take longer to be acted upon.

My family's hard work at that time was continuous. They campaigned for more rehabilitation and, after several attempts, I was admitted to Camden Rehabilitation Centre for therapy every day of the week. After six months of being at home, Camden provided so many, many challenges! First, it has a lot of stairs — and very peculiar stairs, almost between each room — so it forced me to be very active and independent. Also, I met other patients who seemed far worse off than me and many who were far more active, so I found it hard to feel sorry for myself even if I had time! My greatest delight of all was speech therapy with Joan Ellams *twice a day*. We worked on all the problems associated with my basic disorder of dysphasia and dysgraphia.

The weekdays were completely full but I was very happy as I knew my physical independence was increasing. My speech did not show the same improvement but my motivation to keep going stayed strong. At weekends, my mother kept up the pressure, helping every way she could. The biggest problem now was with friends, when they visited. They continually directed all conversation to my mother and not to me, so that mother frequently had to ask them to talk to me. I thought them very rude but it didn't stop me from trying to join in. I started to use the telephone at this time and enjoyed it, even if I could only say 'but, but, but'. Strangely, though, I can often speak better on the phone than face to face with people. The telephone is my lifeline.

As for Camden Rehabilitation Centre, it is a superb place. The staff put themselves second and the patients always come first. I had one whole, lovely year there. I made a little progess with my speech — a tiny amount! Suddenly again I was discharged, but this time we managed to arrange a lot more speech therapy. I knew I was benefiting from speech therapy despite very small gains and I had faith and determination to continue. With all the speech therapists, I could say quite a lot and I wanted to carry on until I could say even more. I wanted to talk to my family and my friends, but my long-term plan was to talk to the public and to the media. My writing is still totally limited to copying, but we found a way round that problem. The Patients Guild from Camden Rehabilitation Centre suggested that I find 'scribes' who worked with me to write to everyone, from friends to the Income Tax. It is a long and complicated business, but it works. The scribes have to work hard to interpret my meaning and it can take up to half an hour to produce the right sentence — the only way is to laugh, make guesses and laugh again, until we find the right words. Using this system, we wrote the letter to the *Daily Telegraph* which began the Speech Clubs. I didn't know how many people had problems like mine but, whatever the number, I was determined to help them and their relatives. Two hundred replies told of as many tragedies. This strengthened my conviction that my stroke was meant to take me into helping others. Later, this same combination of my faith and recognition of the needs of others led to the organisation of the now annual inter-denominational service for people with speech disorders.

The stroke has totally changed my life. I am restricted in many ways; I can't use public transport, so I walk or rely on friends with cars, or taxis. Going to concerts or church services is difficult because I need to spend a penny every half an hour; it's easier not to go! I now visit churches out of service time and pray for a few minutes and my mother and I have communion at home. Being unable to write when I'm by myself is still a great frustration. When I have a good idea I can't jot it down and I may forget by the time a scribe comes. It is difficult to store everything in my head and I dislike not being able to be more systematic.

Despite all the trials, I have continued my campaign for the speech handicapped. I have spoken about the problems and the need for increased speech therapy services on the radio and television several times. I feel it is most vital that doctors, medical students and all paramedical staff know their responsibility to people with speech problems. I am frequently included in lectures to all these groups and, despite some problems with travel, always make this my first priority. I manage to get my message across effectively even though my speech is halting and my sentences may include a jumble of tenses and words which may start off quite mixed up.

I feel frustrated by my lack of fluent speech and writing, every moment of my life. This drives me on to be always doing something for others, as well. So many people have helped me to live a full life again. My mother, my family and my friends, all have shown me incredible love and under-standing. Many speech therapists and all of my scribes have worked hard with me and for me. We may not have a big voice yet, but there's a lot more I want us all to do. I think we *can* do it, as well!

MARY

Mary was born in Newcastle-upon-Tyne in 1907 and lived there until she was 35 years old. She contracted severe polio when she was 3½ and did not go to school until she was 10½. She ran a shorthand and typing school in her own home for fourteen years and then began to get restless and moved to London. She worked at the then Ministry of Works during the day, attending the London School of Economics in the evening where she took her BSc (Economics). She then went on to Birkbeck College, also in the evenings, where she took her MA in Industrial Psychology.

After retirement she campaigned for the acceptance of the disabled into the community and in 1973 she received the Harding Award for her services. She has been honorary director of the Disablement Income Group (DIG), chairman of the Legal and Parliamentary Committee, Central Council for the Disabled, chairman of the Snowden Committee sub-committee dealing with welfare aspects of the integration of the disabled, and founder of the Association of Disabled Professionals. Nowadays she is 'just a private person'.

It all began when I was three and a half years old. Until then I had been just an ordinary little girl. A little girl, not even a tomboy. I was an only child and my mother was 'good with her needle' and so I had pretty clothes. I had fair hair, golden hair, and my mother had a polished round piece of wood about a foot long and an inch in diameter around which strands of hair were brushed when my hair was washed, and again each time it was brushed during the day. And then, suddenly, within in a few hours in fact, my hair was cut off, not bobbed, cut like a boy's and the pretty dresses were never used again. I had contracted polio. Seventy years ago if one had a fever one's hair was cut off: it was assumed, or believed then, that one's hair consumed one's energy, or so the story went. My mother had had her hair cut when she was a little girl when she had scarlet fever.

For some years I was massaged every day with olive-oil — when the polio itself subsided I was completely paralysed — and therefore everything I wore became stained and impregnated with oil, and so I always wore plain white nighties, which soon became browny-grey however well they were washed, and over my nightie I wore a navy blue boy's jersey. It must be remembered that in those days little girls always had long hair and never wore jerseys, and in consequence there were not pretty coloured jerseys.

On one occasion a new doctor came to examine me and in that irritating way grown-ups often speak to children, and indeed often speak to other grown-ups who are sick, he greeted me in jovial tones with, 'Well, my little man, and what are we going to do with you?' Apart from the fact that I didn't want him to do anything with me, doctors always did nasty things, I was outraged at being taken for a little boy. This was the ultimate humiliation for me: I answered, with all the scorn I could muster, 'Mary's a girl's name.'

I still have two photographs, taken about that time, within six months of each other. One shows a robust little girl in a bathing costume with a curl over her left shoulder, hand in hand with two little boys standing on the sands with the sea behind them. The other, the later one, shows a thin little creature sitting in a baby pram in a jersey with cropped hair: surely a peevish little boy? The peevishness wore off with the years, and the hair grew again, but the gold and the curls never returned, it was straight, straight like wire and an indefinite mousey colour. And it was many years before the pretty dresses returned.

No, it was not the paralysis which troubled me, I soon came to terms with that, I soon learned to use whatever was still useable — in my case chiefly my tongue — but I fought desperately to be a LITTLE GIRL. I wasn't a little boy and so I felt in some strange subconscious childish way not exactly sexless, I was too young to realise the significance of that, but a non-person.

There was a little incident which occurred when I was

about seven or eight years old which I didn't fully understand at the time but which made a deep impression on me. I was taken regularly to Mr Ernst, a portly elderly German, who made my steel calipers and steel corset. Because I was growing we had to visit him about three times a year. We had to leave them with him to extend and alter and go every day for a fitting. I liked and respected him. His 'supports' made me much less helpless and equally important he treated me with respect as though I were grown up. One winter my mother was afraid I might feel the cold without my steel corset and so she bought me a little pink corselet trimmed with lace to wear while the other was being altered. When Mr Ernst saw my mother taking the little pink corselet off he blushed and apologised and left the room, saying he'd come back when I was ready. I, of course, couldn't understand what had happened, but I realised that Mr Ernst had acted in a strange manner. When we got home my mother recounted the incident to my father and they both laughed a lot about it, that although Mr Ernst could deal with me naked at times and never bat an eyelid, the sight of feminine pink underclothes embarrassed him. I still didn't understand all this strange grown-up talk and hilarity, but I determined to wear pink underclothes with lace as soon as I was grown up and could buy my own clothes.

When I did grow up I began to realise the disadvantages of being a woman, if one was disabled. I won't elaborate upon the difficulties of menstruation if one is paralysed, because I am sure other contributors will have done this. Also how much easier it is for a man to spend a penny — using a bottle instead of a bed pan. My problem became lack of privacy. Now I know at once others will say but the disabled man is subjected to the same lack of privacy, but is it the same for a man? There is an inherited and built-in secrecy about women's private parts. I have known more than one woman who has delayed going to a doctor until it is too late because she was embarrassed at the very thought of being examined by a man. How often if one enquires

what is the matter with a friend or acquaintance, one is told
with an air of great secrecy, 'I think it is a woman's disease.'
Has one ever heard of a 'man's disease?' But they do have
them. How many women know that feeling when going into
hospital, 'I'm no longer one of the secret society of women,
I'm just a thing.' Your case is unpacked by a nurse: very
kind of her because you can't do it yourself. But nothing
you have is intimate and private, and your body — well,
that's just an object of detached interest, it's no longer
mysterious to those males' eyes examining it, and more
important still it is not desirable, and a good job too in
the circumstances; but will it ever be desirable, will any man
ever again react to it as mysterious and desirable?

Women of my generation were fortunate in one thing
compared to young women today. After the First World
War there were two million surplus women. There were constant references in the 1920s to THE UNEMPLOYED and
THE TWO MILLION SURPLUS WOMEN. No one knew
what to do with them, they were both surplus and they
wouldn't go away. I was one of the surplus women, but
of my half-dozen close friends in adolescence and young
womanhood only one married — there just weren't enough
men to go round — and therefore I felt no stigma that I hadn't
married. It never occurred to me that being an old maid had
anything to do with being disabled. Many disabled girls now
marry, but many don't: it is still easier for a disabled man to
marry than a disabled woman. In many able-bodied women
a disabled husband fulfils a dual purpose, a husband and
someone who is dependent, which women like. But for an
able-bodied man, a wife is, apart from a beloved object, a
status symbol, an added demonstration of his masculinity.
There are of course exceptions, many exceptions, but in
this life it is better to face facts, and the sooner one does so
the more constructive one's life can be.

Names and addresses of organisations

Action for Dysphasic Adults, Northcote House, 37A Royal Street, London SE1 7LL (Tel: 01-261-9572)

Arthritis Care, 6 Grosvenor Crescent, London, SW1X 7ER (Tel: 01-235-0902)

Association of Disabled Professionals, The Stables, 73 Pound Road, Banstead, Surrey SM7 2HV (Tel: Burgh Heath 53366)

Association for Spina Bifida and Hydrocephalus (ASBAH), Tavistock House North, Tavistock Square, London WC1H 9JH (Tel: 01-388-1382)

Association of Sexual and Personal Relationships of the Disabled (SPOD), c/o RADAR, 25 Mortimer Street, London W1N 8AB (Tel: 01-637-5400)

British Deaf Federation, 38, Victoria Place, Carlisle, CA1 1HU (Tel: Carlisle 21088)

British Epilepsy Association, New Wokingham Road, Wokingham, Berks RG11 3AY (Tel: Crowthorne 3122)

British Polio Fellowship, Bell Close, West End Road, Ruislip, Mddx (Tel: Ruislip 75515)

Chest, Heart and Stroke Association, Tavistock House North, Tavistock Square, London, WC1H 9JE (Tel: 01-387-3012)

Disability Alliance, 1 Cambridge Terrace, London NW1 4LJ (Tel: 01-925-4992)

Disablement Income Group (DIG), Attlee House, Toynbee Hall, 28 Commercial Street, London, E1 6LR (Tel: 01-247-2128/6877)

Gemma, B.M. Box 5700, London WC1V 6XX

Greater London Association for Initiatives in Disablement
(GLAID), Flat 4, 188 Ramsden Road, London SW12

*Multiple Sclerosis Society of Great Britain and Northern
Ireland*, 286 Munster Road, London SW6 6AP
(Tel: 01-381-4022/5)

Muscular Dystrophy Group of Great Britain, Natrass House,
35 Macaulay Road, London SW4 0QP (Tel: 01-720-8055)

National Bureau for Handicapped Students, 40 Brunswick
Square, London, WC1N 1AZ (Tel: 01-278-3127)

National Federation of the Blind, 20 Cannon Close, London
SW20 9HA

Physically Handicapped and Able-Bodied (PHAB) 42 Devon-
shire Street, London W1 (Tel: 01-537-7475)

Spastics Society, 12 Park Crescent, London W1N 4EQ
(Tel: 01-636-5020)

Spinal Injuries Association, 5, Crowndale Road, London,
NW1 1TU (Tel: 01-388-6840)